SOUTHERN CALIFORNIA VEGETABLE GARDENING

SOUTHERN CALIFORNIA VEGETABLE GARDENING

JULIE BAWDEN-DAVIS & SABRINA WILDERMUTH

Illustrations by Nicole Kim

SoCal Year-Round Gardening Series

Copyright © 2021 by Julie Bawden-Davis and Sabrina Wildermuth

Cover Illustration by Nicole Kim
Illustrations by Nicole Kim
Graphics by Envato Elements
Photos by Julie Bawden-Davis, Sabrina Wildermuth, Envato Elements, and Dreamstime
Interior and Cover Design by Sabrina Wildermuth and Envato Elements
Roses Are Red Logo Design by Kyle Kane

No part of this book may be reproduced, scanned, or distributed in any printed or electronic form without written permission from the publisher — Roses Are Red Publishing (www.RosesAreRedpublishing.com). Please don't participate in or encourage piracy of copyrighted materials in violation of the authors' rights. Thank you for respecting the hard work of these authors.

All nutritional nuggets are for informational purposes only. You should not rely on this information as a substitute for professional medical advice or treatment. Please consult your personal health-care professional with any questions you may have regarding your own health and diet.

ISBN-13: 978-1-7345012-7-8
ISBN-10: 1-7345012-7-8

Distributed by Roses Are Red Publishing
rosesareredpublishing.com

To Noah: May the days spent in the garden munching on vegetables fill your heart with everlasting peace, joy, and love.

Get All The Good Dirt

Hi Garden Peep!
Thanks for reading. Let's stay in touch. Get cultivated gardening tips for SoCal in Julie's monthly Gardening Peeps newsletter. In addition to insider info on how to grow a lush garden full of tasty produce and beautiful plants, the newsletter includes contests, giveaways, and sneak peeks of upcoming books! Just sign up here:
http://eepurl.com/dIJaV9

Acknowledgments

Many thanks to Chris Roy of the Orange County Farm Supply for his enthusiasm, encouragement, and expert advice. Thank you also to Julie Schlueter for her input and keen eye at proofreading.

Contents

i   Author's Note

01   **Chapter 1**
Vegetable Gardening in SoCal's Unique Climate

13   **Chapter 2**
Feed Your Soil, Feed Your Plants

23   **Chapter 3**
Propagating (AKA Seeding for Veggies)

31   **Chapter 4**
Pests (and Diseases)

43   **Chapter 5**
Growing Lifelong Gardeners

50   **Chapter 6**
Vegetables to Grow in your SoCal Garden

128   About the Authors

131   Index

Southern California Vegetable Gardening

Author's Note

When I began vegetable gardening in earnest in the late 1980s in Southern California, I bought vegetable gardening books and pored over them. At first, I laughed when I read to wait until the danger of frost had passed to plant out certain vegetables, or until the ground was no longer frozen.

After a while, though, I began to get a little irritated when I read things like, no need to water during spring and summer rains. Rain? That sure would be nice, I'd think as I looked out the

December or to be on the lookout for fungal diseases during June Gloom. I read about planting in loamy soil, but found myself trying to break up the clay soil in my yard that I decided was much better suited for building missions.

As generally happens with new gardeners in SoCal, I soon discovered that gardening is unique in this region of ten counties. Here in Southern California, we're blessed to have one of the few Mediterranean climates in the

That's great news, I remember thinking. But what about some guidance for gardening in this ideal climate? I had discovered that while you can grow just about anything in SoCal, that doesn't mean you can simply plant, sit back, and watch an abundant harvest spring forth. At least not without heeding weather variations and giving your plants and your soil some SoCal brand of TLC.

While there were some green gurus back when I started gardening who did take on the task of writing about what to plant when, and I did find help in those pages, I decided to discover the secrets to growing in SoCal myself by writing about gardening for the *Los Angeles Times* Home Design section, which I did for a decade. And because I love strawberries, I wrote the book, *The Strawberry Story: How to Grow Great Berries Year-Round in Southern California*, now in its second edition.

The gardening tips and tricks in this book are meant to help you navigate the SoCal climate so you can have luck the first time you plant Brussels sprouts or carrots. While I'm a big fan of practice teaches you, it can be disappointing when you're excited for a harvest and it doesn't materialize as you'd hoped — or at all. Of course, you're going to have crops that don't do well for you. My intent is that this book gives you a reference that explains any problems you may experience in a way that makes sense and offers solutions.

The chapter on gardening with children features my grandson, Noah. He's growing up in the garden like his mom, Sabrina, my daughter and co-author of this book and series. As a result of having free rein of the vegetable patch, fruit trees, strawberries, and blueberries, Noah's favorite foods are fruits and veggies. Now that he's three, he's also learning to tend his own little garden.

This book and series, which will include future volumes on fruit, flowers, herbs, and small space gardening, has been germinating for quite some time. Sabrina and I began talking about it a couple of years ago. But the seeds were sown back when I was a gardening newbie excited about planting a garden in the SoCal gardening paradise.

Happy Gardening,
Julie Bawden-Davis
Orange, California

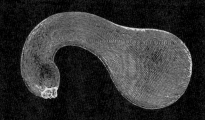

Chapter 1
Vegetable Gardening in SoCal's Unique Climate

Drought, high winds, soaring, searing temperatures, wildfires, and torrential downpours that cause mudslides. SoCal's unique climate is like no other in the world. Of course, those are the downsides. On the upside, Southern California experiences approximately 274 sunny days a year. And a good portion of those days come with mild weather, from the high sixties to the low eighties. Talk about a paradise for plant growth! We do have a cool-season and warm-season here. It's just not as extreme as many other areas of North America. And our coastal regions do experience more cloud cover than inland areas.

Of course, SoCal is experiencing climate change just like other areas of the country and world. According to the US Environmental Protection Agency (EPA), Southern California has warmed about 3 degrees in the last century. Heat waves are becoming more common, as are droughts. Along with drought comes more fuel for wildfires. These are all weather occurrences with which SoCal gardeners must contend.

SoCal and Drought

Drought is cyclical in Southern California, and always has been. However, the length and severity of droughts have increased in recent years. While this doesn't mean that you shouldn't grow vegetables, it does take looking at how you grow them in relation to watering.

Growing vegetables in small spaces, such as raised beds and containers, can save tremendous amounts of water. Though these smaller vessels for growing do require more frequent watering, they need much less water overall. Using methods such as mulching and smart planting in terms of where you locate crops is also helpful, as is planting more trees and using their canopy as shelter in your garden design. Trees transpire, which raises the humidity level in the surrounding area and lowers air temperatures, reducing the need for watering.

In the same respect, vegetable plants will transpire and raise the humidity level in your backyard and create cooler conditions. All of this is good for your yard. Plants can help improve the environment visually, as well as provide oxygen and clean the air we breathe. In short, the more plants you plant, the healthier your air and neighborhood and the planet will be. What better crops to plant than vegetables, which feed us Mother Nature's most wholesome food.

Conserving Water

Drought episodes — especially those that result in water restrictions — bring out ingenuity and resourcefulness amongst gardeners intent on keeping their vegetable gardens watered. Some ways to conserve water so that your vegetable garden remains hydrated include:

Mulching: This refers to covering the soil in the garden bed with organic or inorganic matter that conserves soil moisture and keeps the soil surface cool. Organic mulches are preferred, as they also feed the soil. Common organic mulches include ground, shredded or chipped bark, worm compost, and cocoa mulch. Mulching reduces the need for watering by 35-45 percent.

Small space gardening: When you garden intensively in a small space, you cut down greatly on the need for water. When you do water, you irrigate a much smaller area in terms of square footage. Containers and raised beds, the latter of which are essentially large containers, require regular watering, but the water you apply to them goes directly to plant root zones, rather than to a broad area.

Using gray water: Gray water refers to gently used water coming from sinks, bathtubs, showers, and washing machines. It is not sewage wastewater. Some gardeners use gray water to irrigate their gardens. If you decide to do this, keep some cautionary tips in mind. Because you are generally

Vegetable Gardening in SoCal's Unique Climate

washing items like yourself, dishes and clothing in gray water, it will contain trace amounts of detergents, as well as food, grease, and hair. For this reason, it's important that you use products free of chlorine, salt, and boron, or the gray water could harm your soil and plants. When watering vegetable plants with gray water, avoid wetting the fruit and foliage.

Unused drinking water: If you and those in your household drink water on a regular basis, you may find that you end up with half-empty water glasses and bottles sitting about. Use this water on your vegetable garden. Related to this, when you're waiting for water to heat up for washing dishes and the like, catch that water and use it to water plants.

Rain barrels: When SoCal does have rain, catching this elixir in rain barrels is highly advised. Ensure that the rain barrel you use has a fine screen that is mosquito-proof. If you can attach your rain barrel to a downspout that will ensure that you collect a great deal of water in a short period of time. If this isn't possible, the rain barrel will still collect water for you. You can also simply put out an open vessel during a rainstorm to collect water. Just make sure to use the water within two to three days, or it may become a mosquito breeding ground.

Watering Basics

When it comes to gardening, watering often causes the most head scratching. To water or not? That is truly an age-old gardening question. The answers aren't always straightforward. Your best bet is to find out what each vegetable plant requires in terms of watering and then water accordingly.

A good tool for measuring the moisture in soil is a moisture meter. This pronged instrument is inserted into the soil. You are then given a scientific answer as to when it's time to water. These instruments use electrical currents to determine the moisture content in the soil. Readings tend to show on a scale of 1-10, with 10 being very wet and 1 being completely dry. Generally speaking, you'll want to keep most vegetable plant soil in the moist range of 4-6 on the moisture meter scale.

Chapter 1

Moisture Meter

At the same time, getting to know a plant and how it responds when you water or don't water also helps you determine water readiness. That means that it does take a bit of intuitive knowingness when it comes to watering. The more experience you have with watering, the better you'll get at what is truly a gardening art.

Weather Fluctuations

SoCal's unique gardening climate comes with its own set of weather challenges. We may not have to "batten down the hatches" for hurricanes or tornadoes or prepare for hard frosts and inches of snow, but we do have drying Santa Ana winds with which to contend. Relative humidity can dip 30-40 percentage points in as little as 20 minutes when the Santa Anas come calling.

And when the sky finally opens and rain comes pouring down — especially after months of drought — there will be flooding and erosion in the SoCal garden. Add to this the occasional overnight freeze, and you've got some anticipating and planning to do. Temperature fluctuations will affect the growth of your vegetable garden.

When the Winds Blow

The Santa Ana winds and dry, windy, hot weather in general can wreak havoc on the vegetable garden — especially during the cool season. You may have a cauliflower plant that is thriving in January, and then one hot, windy day signals to the plant that the cool season is over and it's time to bolt (flower) and stop producing. Because most of a plants' sugars are required to make those flowers, the fruit and foliage is left tasting bitter. If a cool-season plant like cauliflower begins flowering, harvest immediately— no matter its size, and enjoy it.

The Santa Ana winds, which are exclusive to Southern California and hit October through April, can blow at 30 to 40 miles per hour and even sometimes top 50 miles per hour. Winds of that velocity do a great deal of damage to plants, including uprooting them, stripping off leaves, and burning foliage. Burned foliage shows up 3 to 4 days after the windstorm in the form of browned leaf edges and tips. The drying winds will also suck moisture out of the soil, dehydrating your landscape. Container and raised bed plants will perish quickly, if you don't water them promptly, which often means during the windstorm.

Fortunately, you can often minimize the damage from hot, windy weather and get your vegetable garden through a bout of unseasonable weather. Misting the garden periodically during a windstorm or on a hot day can humidify the garden and bring down the temperature just enough that the plants don't get the message to bolt and shut down production. If you're growing in containers, pull them to safety indoors or against the house under the eaves. When you know the winds are coming, soak the vegetable garden well. That way in-ground and raised bed plants will be better able to stand up to the drying winds.

When it Pours

When it rains in California, as the song goes, it pours. Man, it pours. And pours. And pours. And our dry ground isn't used to the wet. That means you soon have pools or even lakes of water in your landscape. Watch the rain come down on your veggie garden, and you might begin to wonder just how much it can take.

First of all, plants can take quite a bit of rain. Secondly, rain is a gift from the sky in terms of leaching harmful salts deeper into the soil away from plant roots. Rain also contains a dilute form of nitric acid, which is a natural form of fertilizer that will make your veggie plants perk up. And if thunder and lightning occurs, the rain's beneficial effects are even more potent. You'll often find that after a rainstorm your vegetable garden will look healthier.

Of course, if your garden is under a few feet of water for any length of time, your plants will show the effects. Leaves may yellow and die back, and buds, blooms and fruits may drop off. Root rot may also set in a week or so after heavy rains.

Chapter 1

If standing water in your garden is excessive, you've likely got a drainage problem. With minor drainage situations, you can dig trenches prior to the next rainstorm that will direct water to flow away from plants. Major problems will require installing an underground drainage system in your landscape.

Other ways to get around water damage to your vegetable garden include planting in containers and raised beds, which both drain much more readily than ground soil. If you wish to continue planting in the ground, do so on mounds in the future. Mulching also helps to absorb rainwater and prevent erosion.

When it Freezes

It doesn't happen that often in most areas of SoCal, but occasionally we'll get winter nights that dip below freezing for a time. Fortunately, this is welcomed by many vegetable plants in the *Brassica* family. For instance, kale, cauliflower, and cabbage taste even better after a touch of frost.

If you're growing something out of season, which is entirely possible in our mild climate — like tomatoes — even an hour of below freezing weather will do permanent damage. A serious frost can affect plant tissue and even kill a plant. Tropical plants like tomatoes and peppers will freeze and literally turn to mush after a hard frost. Depending on severity, some plants may collapse, while others will lose leaves. If there is fruit on the plant, it may freeze and become inedible. If there are buds, flowers, or young fruit, it may fall off.

To help prevent frost damage, there are several things you can do:

Keep plants well watered: Frost damages plants by dehydrating them. That means if you have your vegetable plants adequately hydrated prior to frost, they will be a lot less likely to sustain damage.

Use an anti-transpirant: These products are applied to the leaf surface. They cut down on a plant's water loss through the leaves. (This product is also helpful for windy conditions.)

Protect plants: Make a protective tent over your vegetable garden. This requires creating a structure that

Vegetable Gardening in SoCal's Unique Climate

doesn't touch any parts of the plants. Foliage touched by the covering will be in contact with outside temperatures and can sustain damage. Use an old sheet, burlap, or frost blanket designed for this purpose. Hang the covering over a frame made out of wood or PVC piping. For a quick cover for small plants, place a cardboard box over the plant you want to protect.

Move potted plants: Pull containerized veggie plants to safety inside a garage or under an eave or patio cover. Heat radiates off the house, so the closer you can put the container to the house, the better.

Choose your planting location carefully: Avoid placing frost-sensitive vegetable plants in the lowest area of your yard, as this is generally the coldest spot. Out in the open is another cold spot. (See "Take Advantage of Microclimates" for warm locations in your garden.)

Take Advantage of Microclimates

In addition to the SoCal overall climate, every home landscape has a variety of unique microclimates. These include sunnier and shadier spots, as well as warmer and cooler areas.

Microclimates arise in a landscape in response to a variety of environmental conditions. Lots vary in size and shape and in their location in relation to the sun. Many yards have trees and nearby structures such as patio covers and awnings that cast shade.

Becoming familiar with the warmest and coolest, and sunniest and shadiest, areas of your yard allows you to determine what vegetable plants to plant where. Here are some environmental situations that cause significant differences in temperature and lighting. This information can help you find the ideal spots for your vegetable plants.

Examine the directionality of your house. Make a diagram of your house and label each side. Then consider:

- Western-facing walls in full sun will be hot and harsh. This effect is

Chapter 1

exponential when the wall is white. If there are nearby trees that shade the area at some point during the day, this effect will be minimized. Such locations are ideal for growing crops that require a lot of heat, including tomatoes in the wintertime. It is also an ideal spot for heat-loving plants when growing vegetables along the coast.

- Southern-facing walls in full sun will be warm, yet less harsh than western-facing. Such a location will also provide warmth for plants at night, especially if the walls are white. This is a good spot for most vegetable plants, including a winter tomato crop.
- Eastern-facing walls get sun until midday and are then cast into shade. These are ideal locations for vegetable plants that can grow in partial sun.
- North-facing walls are the darkest and coldest. Such areas aren't a good location for growing most vegetable plants.
- Look for hot spots in the lawn. Browning grass can indicate that an area is reflecting sun off a window. This spot will get especially hot during the day.
- Consider trees. Trees drink a great deal of water. Keep that in mind if your raised bed or in-ground garden is located near trees. Trees will also shade a nearby garden at different times throughout the day and throughout the seasons. The more a tree grows, the more shade it will cast.
- Use an outdoor thermometer to gauge the temperature in different areas of your yard throughout the day and evening.

Growing out of Season

The benefit of our unseasonably warm weather is that you can push the proverbial green envelope and grow many crops out of season. One popular crop to grow during our cool season is tomatoes. See next page for tips on growing your own winter crop.

Vegetable Gardening in SoCal's Unique Climate

Winter Tomatoes

The key to successful fall and winter tomato harvests is choosing the right tomato varieties and following a few cool-season tomato growing tips.

Tomato varieties that do well in our cooler months set fruit even when nighttime temperatures dip below 50 degrees. Some varieties that fit this profile include heirlooms such as Abe Lincoln, Box Car Willy, Marianna's Peace, Japanese Black, Stupice, and Thessaloniki. In hybrids, some good choices are Celebrity, Champion, Early Cascade, Early Girl, Oregon Spring, Patio, Sungold, and Super Sweet 100.

To enjoy an abundant tomato harvest in fall and winter when everyone else is resorting to store-bought, tasteless tomatoes, keep the following growing tips in mind:

- Plant while the weather and ground is still warm, which gives tomato plants a chance to set down an extensive, strong root system. Good planting times are September and October.
- Choose a warm, full-sun location with protection from winds. An ideal location is up against the house on a west- or south-facing wall, or against a brick wall. Homes and brick walls radiate heat, which helps tomato plants thrive and produce even when temperatures dip. Don't plant the tomato in an unprotected, low area of the yard, as it will get too cold and won't bear well.
- Plant in well-drained soil. Improve drainage, if necessary, by amending with a 2- to 3-inch layer of compost and pumice.
- Plant deep. Pinch off the bottom one to five leaves at the stem, making sure to leave at least one set of leaves at the top. Bury the stem in soil to just above the last notch left from leaf removal. If the stem is straight, bury the plant straight into the ground. If the stem is bent, bury on its side. (See illustration below.) Roots will emerge from the notches, creating a stronger plant.

Chapter 1

- Water well after planting and mulch to conserve moisture and nutrients. Mulching with products such as shredded bark protects your plants from drying Santa Ana winds common in the fall and winter. Layering on mulch also promotes the growth of beneficial bacteria in the soil.
- Water when the first 3 to 4 inches of soil has dried. When the tomato is newly transplanted, this usually means watering every day, then every other day, and then easing off until you water just once a week. Overwatering leads to watery fruit and can cause fungal diseases like root rot, especially during cool weather. Refrain from watering during rainy periods.
- Feed with an organic tomato food at the time of planting. Such a fertilizer will be low in nitrogen. Excess nitrogen leads to lush foliage and little to no fruit.
- Provide adequate growing room. Space plants 4 to 5 feet apart in tomato cages.
- Keep tomato plants as warm as possible during especially nippy weather by using products such as wall o' water, available at nurseries and through home supply stores. When the temperatures are going to dip below freezing, (which occurs a handful of nights a year in SoCal), cover the tomato cage with a frost blanket, available at nurseries and home and garden centers.
- Growing in containers is ideal for winter tomatoes because in the event of frost, you can move the pots to a sheltered location such as under a patio covering, next to the house, or indoors for the night. To successfully grow in pots, choose small to medium-sized tomato varieties. Provide containerized tomato plants with a soil that is water retaining, yet drains well.

Vegetable Gardening in SoCal's Unique Climate

June Gloom

It might not be great beach weather, but June Gloom isn't all that bad for plants. As a matter of fact, the mild weather gives the veggies you planted in May a chance to develop really strong root systems. Overcast days also offer pleasant gardening weather. Take the opportunity to do some heavy lifting in the garden before hot days set in. Clear away cool-season vegetable garden debris, add compost to the soil, and mulch.

Problems that may arise as a result of June Gloom include overwatering. Because the days are cooler and the sun is not as strong and bright, plants will transpire (their way of sweating) much less quickly than when the sun is strong. That means your vegetable plants won't be drinking as much as when the days are hot and bright. Keep that in mind and avoid overwatering.

Additionally, June Gloom creates favorable conditions for foliage leaf diseases, such as Leaf Spot and Downy and Powdery Mildew. Avoid watering foliage when irrigating your vegetable garden during June Gloom. This will help prevent foliar disease. Also prune off infected leaves as they appear and dispose of them to avoid spread.

Coastal Gardening

The maritime influence that includes milder temperatures and a greater incidence of cloudy days compared to the rest of SoCal gives vegetable gardening along the coast its own set of challenges and benefits. While there are many crops that can be grown year-round along the coast, such as artichokes and leafy greens like lettuce and Swiss chard, and root crops like carrots and beets, heat-lovers don't thrive as well as their inland counterparts. And though cooler temperatures thanks to cloud cover and seabreezes are common, frost is generally unheard of. That means that

Chapter 1

crops that like a kiss of frost like Brussels sprouts may not get the cold weather they need to thrive.

On the plus side, milder weather means less frequent watering and fewer chances of losing plants as you might on a hot inland day. Despite some growing limitations along the coast, it's possible to grow a lush vegetable garden that supplies you with a bounty of produce — all enjoyed amidst a pleasant ocean breeze.

Vegetable Gardening in SoCal's Unique Climate

Chapter 2
Feed Your Soil, Feed Your Plants

Although we tend to focus on plants, soil health should be top priority. Roots live in the soil, and they are the life force of every plant. Care for the soil and you care for the roots. Without thriving roots, you won't have healthy vegetable plant foliage, flowering, or fruiting. (According to Merriam-Webster, "anything that grows on a plant and is the means by which that plant gets its seeds out into the world is a fruit", so the reference of fruit in this book refers to vegetables.)

A healthy soil contains a high degree of beneficial microorganisms, including bacteria and fungi. Millions of microorganisms living in soil accomplish a variety of important tasks. These include digesting and converting various raw materials, such as fertilizer, into a form that plants can take up by their roots. Healthy soil contains a balance of air space that allows for bacteria growth. Such soil also contains worms and their nutritive castings (poop). Rich soil crumbles when you till it, and water penetrates easily. If this doesn't sound like your soil, don't worry. Much of SoCal has clay soil, with areas along the coast often having sandy soil.

Southern California's Clay Soil

Clay soil common in SoCal is tightly bound, featuring very small pore space, which offers very little room for water and air penetration. That makes it difficult for bacteria to thrive and roots to grow. Such soil will become crusty and very hard when dry, making it nearly impossible for many plants to grow. On the plus side, clay soil tends to be rich in nutrients. That means if you work with clay soil by adding amendments, you can create a soil for strong growth.

Amending Clay Soil

Clay can be amended with certain materials to create an environment more hospitable to vegetable growing.

Compost is a good addition to soil, providing much-needed air space while also adding nutrients to the soil. Use either homemade or bagged compost. (See composting method on the next page for easily making your own).

To add compost to soil, pour the compost on top of the planting area you wish to amend. Generally, you want to apply a 2- to 5-inch layer, depending on what you're planting. Then mix the compost into the top 2 to 12 inches of soil. How deep you dig the compost in will depend on the crop you're planting and how deep its roots grow.

Another good choice for amending clay soil is pumice. This porous, igneous rock is an ideal amendment for creating fast drainage, which most vegetable plants require. Unlike perlite, which is widely used as a draining agent in potting soils, pumice has some weight to it, so it won't wash away or break down. Add pumice to your planting area, and it will remain there. How much pumice you add will depend on how poor the drainage is. It's generally a good idea to start with a 2-inch layer of pumice. Work it into the soil and test the drainage. (See next section). If the drainage is still poor, add another 1-inch layer and repeat the test.

Drainage Test

A good way to test the drainage in your garden is to do a drainage test. This refers to digging a hole 10 to 12 inches deep and filling it with water. If the hole drains within thirty minutes, the area has good drainage. If it takes an hour, the drainage is mediocre. If it takes more than an hour to drain, the drainage is poor in that area. Most vegetable plants will perish with what is known as "wet feet", referring to continually wet roots. Until you amend and create faster drainage in an area, it's best not to plant vegetables there.

Amending Sandy Soil

Sandy soil common in SoCal coastal regions has very little binding or water retention ability. The particle sizes in sandy soil create much larger pore spaces than clay soil, resulting in a lot of air space and fast drainage. That means water and fertilizer quickly wash through, leaving vegetable plants parched and without nutrients. To vegetable garden successfully in sandy soil, it's necessary to amend. Adding compost will bind up the air space to a level where the soil retains moisture and nutrients.

Feed Your Soil, Feed Your Plants

Easy Composting

In many SoCal gardens, it's difficult to fit the standard-sized compost bin into the landscape. This is especially the case with systems that have several compartments. There are composter tumblers that work well. With these you fill them and turn them. For an even simpler method that you can wedge into tight spaces, try composting in a plastic trash can.

Here are the steps to create the composter pictured to the right:

1. Use a sharp instrument like an ice pick to make a bunch of holes in the lid and sides of the trashcan, about every 3-4 inches.
2. Put the trashcan in an area that gets bright light. It can go in direct sunlight during the cool months, but place the bin in some shade during the hot summer months.
3. Put into the trashcan equal parts dry (carbon) ingredients, like dried leaves and ground up stems/branches, along with wet (nitrogen) ingredients like vegetable and fruit scraps and lawn clippings (as long as you don't treat your lawn with pesticides and it isn't full of weeds.)
4. Add a bag of composted chicken manure or compost starter.
5. Wet the contents to moisten and mix ingredients well.
6. Put the lid on the trashcan.
7. Mix periodically or let it sit. The more you mix, the sooner it will make compost for you.
8. Enjoy some nutritive compost for your plants!

Soil for Containers and Raised Beds

When growing in pots and raised beds, it's important to use a high-quality, organic potting soil that drains well, yet is moisture retentive, which also means that the soil is able to retain nutrients. Many commercial

Chapter 2

mixes are very "barky", consisting primarily of ground-up bark. Such "potting soil" is not a good choice for container and raised bed gardening. It won't hold onto water or nutrients.

Choose instead a potting soil that contains peat moss or coconut coir and vermiculite, which promote water and nutrient retention, and perlite or pumice for drainage. Other good organic ingredients include worm castings (vermicompost), bat and bird guano, feather meal, fish meal, alfalfa meal, bonemeal, and bloodmeal.

Humus is Key to Alive Soil

One major key to creating a rich, active soil for your vegetable plants is humus. This soft, brown-black substance forms in the last stages of decomposition of vegetable or animal matter and is the lifeblood of nature. Rich in nutrients and organic matter, humus creates an environment that supports and encourages beneficial soil bacteria and fungi. Humus also helps plants absorb nutrients more efficiently by making various minerals more readily available.

We can thank humus for our forests and jungles. This rich, organic substance is the reason wild plants grow on their own without outside help like pre-packaged fertilizer. Of course, potted plants and raised beds require human intervention. They're depending on you to mimic nature. Applying humus in the form of humic acid is one of the best ways to accomplish this. Humic acid comes in granular and liquid form.

Mulching Feeds and Protects Soil

Mulching and the resulting decomposition of organic matter leads to the constant production of humus. Mulch also keeps important soil organisms safe, simultaneously increasing the disease resistance of your plants. According to research, microorganisms in mulch produce enzymes and other chemicals that stimulate plants to develop systemic acquired resistance (SAR) to some plant diseases. Mulch also shelters the soil from temperature variations. The more constant the soil temperature, the faster your plants will grow and produce. Mulch also cuts down on watering by as much as 45 percent.

When you apply mulch, you replicate what occurs in nature. In the forest, the ground is littered with fallen vegetation that insulates and feeds trees and other plants. Plant-derived mulches, such as bark, cocoa mulch, coir, straw, and compost, are the best mulching choices. These substances feed the soil and keep the planting area cool and moist.

Compost with Worm Castings

If you lack the room to do traditional composting, you could try worm farming. Vermicomposting is a great way to create compost in a small space. This refers to using red worms to compost kitchen waste and dry plant materials to make black, earthy-smelling, nutrient-rich humus perfect for use as a fertilizer and soil amendment. The worms actually do all of the work for you. You simply feed them table scraps and yard waste, and they produce nutrient-rich castings (a delicate way of saying worm poop). Though it sounds like a messy proposition, worms can actually boast that their excretions don't stink! They will noiselessly convert mounds of kitchen scraps like coffee grounds and vegetable trimmings into a rich, nearly odorless soil amendment. If you are squeamish about worms, skip worm farming and buy already prepared worm castings.

Good Fungus

Mention the word fungus to many gardeners, and they think of root rot. The truth is, some fungus is beneficial,

Chapter 2

such as mycorrhizae. These beneficial fungi form a symbiotic relationship with plants by attaching to their roots and bringing in more nutrients and water than a plant can on its own. They also make plants stronger and disease-resistant. High-quality potting soils contain mycorrhizae, so look for this ingredient when purchasing soil. Mycorrhizae are also sold separately in a dry form that can be applied to the root zone.

To have luck using mycorrhizal products, it's important to use organic fertilizers because chemical fertilizers inhibit the fungus. When a plant has a fast food diet of quickly absorbable fertilizer, it fails to activate the mycorrhizal fungi spores, which simply stay dormant. For best results, mycorrhizae should be applied at the root zone of the plant, which you can do by either transplanting or making chambers in the soil with a pencil or wooden dowel and putting the mycorrhizae in the holes. Work the dowel down 2 to 3 inches and pour fertilizer in each hole.

Why Soil pH Matters

When a plant is ailing and produces stunted, weak growth despite proper care, the soil's pH may be the culprit. This degree of acidity or alkalinity is one of the last things gardeners check, but it should be one of the first. Many plant health problems are not caused by disease, insects, or nutritional deficiencies, but rather by soil that is too acid or alkaline. Soil pH is vital to vegetable plant health. If it is too low or too high, many nutrients cannot be released to the plants. A common example of this is phosphorus, which needs a pH near neutral to be available. Without this essential nutrient, plants can't perform various important functions, such as photosynthesis and root formation and growth. Other important nutrients that can get tied up in soil when the pH is off are calcium, magnesium, and nitrogen.

Here's an example of how incorrect soil pH can cause a problem for your vegetable garden. Blossom end rot is a condition in tomatoes that causes the bottom of the tomato to rot and turn mushy. This is caused by a calcium deficiency in the soil. One way to rectify the calcium deficiency is to add gypsum to the soil. However, if the soil pH is off, the calcium in the gypsum won't be available to the plant, and the blossom end rot will continue.

Soil pH can also have an effect on the activity of soil microorganisms such as fungi and bacteria. A pH reading that is too high or low will lead to a loss of these microorganisms, which results in a less healthy soil overall.

Soil pH is fairly easy to understand: It refers to a scale of acidity-alkalinity that ranges from 0 to 14, with the most common levels found between 4 and 8. Seven is neutral. Readings above 7 show alkalinity; readings below show acidity. Each full point up or down the scale represents a tenfold increase or decrease in the degree of soil acidity and alkalinity. For example, a soil with a pH of 6 has 10 times more acid than one with a pH of 7, and soil with a pH of 5 is 100 times more acidic than the 7 soil. With this in mind, a full point change can mean the difference between life and death for certain plants.

SoCal soil tends to be alkaline. Our water is also on the alkaline side. Alkaline water can raise pH, and so can some fertilizers. You can lower pH by adding soil sulfur to your garden soil, containers or raised beds. (In the unlikely event you need to raise your soil pH in SoCal, you would amend with dolomite lime or oyster shell).

Some vegetable plants, like peanuts, prefer things on the acidic side, which may be difficult to deliver if you plant in the ground in SoCal. That's where raised beds and containers come in handy. It's much easier to control soil pH in these containerized growing situations.

Checking Your Soil's pH

Test kits and meters are available for checking soil pH. Keep in mind that pH meters require occasional calibration, and accurate models will be more expensive. Soil test kits are less expensive, and accurate. To test your soil pH, gather several soil samples from the vegetable planting area. Air dry the soil before testing. Water is used in the testing process. You need water that is neutral pH, or your results will be skewed. Distilled water is a good choice. Follow the soil testing kit directions carefully to ensure an accurate result.

Feed with Organic Fertilizers

Quick-acting synthetic fertilizers that promise a miracle in the garden can lead to a disaster with vegetable gardens. Such foods cause rapid foliar growth at the expense of the plant's root system. That means you'll get a lot of foliage but little flowering and fruiting. A plant that is unbalanced with more foliage than roots becomes a target for pests and diseases. When used in containers and raised beds, artificial fertilizers sterilize potting soil by killing beneficial fungi and soil microbes, further weakening plants.

If you take a natural approach to feeding your vegetable garden with organic fertilizers, you nourish the plants in your garden. Organic fertilizers provide your vegetable plants with a gentle, slow-release, continuous feeding. Signs that plants may need fertilizing include yellowing leaves, less new growth, and little to no flowering or fruiting. Keep in mind that overwatering can also cause these signs, so check that you aren't overwatering for the plant type.

Liquid fertilizer provides a fast and easy way to feed your vegetable plants. You simply mix the fertilizer into water, according to package directions; then pour it on. Avoid wetting foliage when watering with fertilizer solution.

When fertilizing with granular fertilizer, it's important to get the food to the root zone of the plant. To quickly and efficiently fertilize, use a wooden dowel or similar object and make holes in the soil surrounding the plant, 2 to 4 inches deep, every 3 to 4 inches. Fill the holes with a small amount of granular fertilizer. Refill the holes with soil and water well. If the planting area is dry, water first to moisten; then apply fertilizer and water again after application.

Feed Your Soil, Feed Your Plants

What is N-P-K?

The set of three hyphenated numbers on a fertilizer bottle or bag signifies the analysis of the food. These numbers stand for the nitrogen, phosphorus, and potassium content of the fertilizer. Commonly referred to as N-P-K, these nutrients are found in complete organic fertilizers and are critical to plant growth. The first letter stands for nitrogen, which is key to chlorophyll production. Nitrogen keeps foliage green. The second letter signifies phosphorus. This mineral promotes sturdy cell structure, healthy root growth, and abundant flowering and fruiting. The third letter, K, stands for potassium. This mineral plays a role in photosynthesizing, as well as nutrient and water management. Potassium also strengthens plants against pests and diseases.

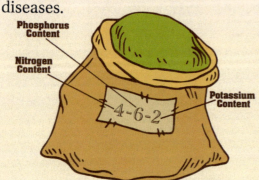

In addition to the three major nutrients, plants also need micronutrients such as calcium, magnesium, sulfur, iron, and zinc.

Choose Organic Fertilizers

Fortunately, it's fairly easy to spot organic fertilizer. Just look for a low N-P-K ratio. Those foods that have numbers less than 10 are often organic. Something like a 20-20-20 is generally a synthetic mix and should be avoided. Though it might seem like a good idea to give a plant as much of a nutrient as possible — more is not better. Mixes with a high concentration of synthetic nutrients destroy precious soil microbes and fungi. Ironically, plants absorb very little nutrition from such high-powered foods.

Good organic fertilizers are products of natural decomposition and are easy for plants to digest. They are derived from simple sources that come from the earth. You should recognize them and their ingredients. Carefully read the labels on your fertilizer bottles and bags. Choose products with nutrients in their elemental form (remember the periodic table of elements you learned in high school).

The fertilizers in the following list feed plants as well as the soil.

Chapter 2

Organic Fertilizers List

- **Alfalfa meal** [Natural growth stimulant; plus trace minerals]
- **Bat and bird guano** [Nitrogen & calcium]
- **Bloodmeal** [Nitrogen]
- **Bonemeal** [Phosphorus, calcium, & trace minerals]
- **Chicken manure** [Nitrogen]
- **Cottonseed meal** [Nitrogen; phosphorus; potassium; also acidifies soil]
- **Epsom salts** [Magnesium]
- **Feather meal** [Nitrogen]
- **Fish emulsion** [Nitrogen, phosphorus, potassium, & trace minerals]
- **Fish meal** [Nitrogen, phosphorus, & potassium]
- **Greensand** [Calcium, iron, magnesium, potassium, & trace minerals]
- **Gypsum** [Calcium & sulfur]
- **Humic acids** [Organic matter & trace minerals]
- **Kelp meal** [Potassium & trace minerals]
- **Langbeinite** [Potassium, magnesium, & sulfur]
- **Oyster shells** [Calcium]
- **Rock phosphate** [Phosphorus]
- **Seaweed** [Trace minerals & natural growth hormones]
- **Shrimp Meal** [Nitrogen, phosphorus, & calcium]
- **Soft Rock Phosphate** [Phosphorus & calcium]
- **Worm castings/Vermicompost** [Trace minerals]

Feed Your Soil, Feed Your Plants

Chapter 3
Propagating (AKA Seeding for Veggies)

While buying transplants from the nursery is easy and expedient, at some point you'll want to grow vegetables you can't find in the nursery or home and garden center. In the case of root vegetables like carrots and beets, you'll need to plant from seed in order to grow these veggies.

The world of seed starting is a fun and fascinating one. Planting a seed and spying a tiny plant peeking through the soil is an exciting, fulfilling experience. Few things are more satisfying in the gardening world than watching a tiny seedling grow and produce. A homegrown veggie you tended from birth has the best taste you can ever imagine.

Good Reasons for Seeding

Plant from seed and you can grow unusual or hard to find vegetables. Seed catalogues are full of possibilities. Your challenge will be deciding what type of tomato you'd like to try, or cucumber, or beet, or broccoli, or kale. The list goes on.

If you seed your own plants, you can also oversee their care. This is especially important if you wish to garden organically. Growing from seed enables you to ensure that your plants are never treated with pesticides. This is especially an issue for leaf crops such as kale and lettuce.

You'll also save money when you grow from seed. A packet of seeds costs about the same as just one vegetable plant in the nursery or home and garden store.

Open-Pollinated vs. Hybrid Seed

You may have heard the terms hybrid seed and open-pollinated. And you may have even been told to plant one or the other. To clear up any confusion, here is an explanation of these two types of seeds.

Hybrid Seed

A hybrid seed is the first generation (F-1) seed of a cross between two parents of the same type of plant. For instance, breeders will cross two tomato varieties. Why bother crossing plants? Hybridizers do this to get a better plant. For instance, they will cross a tomato with disease resistance with another tomato that grows large fruit. It may be that the tomato that grows large fruit is susceptible to disease, so when this cross is accomplished, you get a plant that produces a big tomato and resists common tomato diseases (of which there are many.)

That sounds great, doesn't it? In fact, it is great. If you are intent on growing really big tomatoes without interference from a pesky disease, for instance, then this would be the ideal type of seed for you to grow in your home garden. With an 'Early Girl' tomato, for instance, you can expect a good-sized tomato that produces early in the season every time.

Some vegetables, such as beans, lettuce and peas, aren't generally hybridized, but many are. One of the first hybridized vegetables was a tomato back in the late 1940s. W. Atlee Burpee & Co. created the 'Big Boy' tomato. Burpee, the founder of the company, named the vegetable after his baby son.

At that time, the horticultural community thought hybridizing was a trend that wouldn't last or extend beyond the home market. Obviously, they were mistaken. Traits such as reliable production, disease resistance, and uniform looks made hybrids quickly popular. Today, a majority of commercial crops are hybrid. If it weren't for hybridizing, we wouldn't have the many improved plants that we have. This includes traits that allow for growing in wider geographic regions.

Like all good things, there are drawbacks, however. One of the biggest drawbacks is that the fruit from hybrid plants doesn't produce viable seed. The traits produced in the plant are only uniform in that first generation of seed. That means you need to buy more of those seeds if you want the same crop.

Propagating (AKA Seeding for Vegetables)

Open-Pollinated (OP) Seed

Open-pollinated seed is the type of seed that has produced plants since the beginning of time. Such seed is pure, meaning there is no crossing that has taken place through manmade hybridization. Such seed does have the ability to cross-pollinate on its own through wind and pollinators, but the seed produces the same plants genetically.

Open-pollinated seed and the vegetables this seed produces have stood the test of time. When you plant an OP tomato seed, for instance, you know you're planting the same seed that our ancestors did.

For a diverse, reliable vegetable garden that produces throughout the year, many gardeners choose to reap the benefits of growing both hybrid and OP seed. Hybrids offer disease resistance and reliability, while OP varieties give you an adventure every time you stick a seed in soil.

What About Non-GMO Seed?

You may have been urged to only grow non-GMO seed, but do you know what this means? First, it is important to understand that GMOs are not the same as the hybrid plants previously described. Hybrid seeds are created by a pollen exchange between two plants within the same species. This is done by human hands crossing pollen in a garden or field environment. Whereas GMO seeds are genetically engineered by modifying the genes in a laboratory from a species unrelated to the plant at-hand.

You do not have to worry about genetically modified seeds in your home garden, as there are currently no genetically modified seeds available to the general public. While there are GMO crops grown in the US, these are production crops such as soy, canola, sugar beets, and field corn. Fewer than 10 genetically modified species are available as fresh produce.

Seeding Indoors

Except for root crops, it's possible to seed most vegetables indoors for transplanting outdoors later. This is a good practice if you are trying to get transplants ready to plant at the ideal time in the garden. For instance, you

Chapter 3

can plant cool-season crops like Brussels sprouts and cauliflower indoors in August and transplant in the garden in mid-September.

Young, tender seedlings are also magnets for various pests. Seeding indoors allows you to wait until the plants are bigger and stronger before transplanting.

Steps to seeding indoors:
1. Use a seed starting tray that contains drainage holes.
2. Fill the tray with 2 to 3 inches of damp, lightweight seed starting mix.
3. Sprinkle seed on the top of the seed starting mix. Cover with a fine layer of more seed starting mix (oftentimes the seed packet will tell you how deep to plant the seeds; bigger seeds need a thicker layer of soil than small seeds).
4. Spray the top of the soil with a fine mist of water to completely wet the soil.
5. Cover the seed starting tray to hold in moisture and hasten germination. Many seed starting kits come with a clear plastic cover. Or cover with plastic wrap. Remove cover/wrap once seedlings emerge and begin to reach cover.
6. Keep the soil moist but not soggy while the seeds germinate. If allowed to dry out, the little seedlings may die. Once seedlings emerge, also keep them moist at all times.
7. Seedlings require bright lighting to thrive. Once seedlings begin growing, place them in a location with bright light. An unobstructed eastern or southern windowsill will work well during the spring and summer months, but it may not provide enough light in the fall and winter months. When window lighting is limited, place the plants under full-spectrum lighting positioned 2 to 3 inches above the plants. You will know the seedlings aren't getting enough light if they become leggy and lean toward the light. Leggy seedlings often produce weak plants that may never grow to maturity and produce a crop.
8. Thin seedlings to 1 to 2 inches apart once they've developed their second set of true leaves. The first rounded leaves they develop are cotyledons. These will eventually fall off and true leaves will develop. If the plants start to outgrow the tray and it's not time to plant outdoors, transplant into small individual pots.

Propagating (AKA Seeding for Vegetables)

Seeding into Trays

Seedlings under Full-Spectrum Light

Hardening Off

When you grow seedlings indoors for transplanting in the garden, it's important to do what is known as hardening them off. This refers to slowly acclimating them to the outdoors, so they don't go into shock when you plant them.

Begin hardening off seedlings once they reach 2 to 3 inches tall and the weather is warm or cool enough to plant that particular crop. Harden off over a 7-day period. Here is a suggested schedule:

Day 1: Place plants outside in the morning until early afternoon in an area that receives dappled sunlight or bright shade. Bring plants back indoors.

Day 2: Place plants outside in the morning until late afternoon in an area that receives dappled sunlight or bright shade. Bring plants back indoors.

Day 3: Place plants outside in the morning until evening in an area that receives dappled sunlight or bright shade. Bring plants back indoors.

Day 4: Place plants outside in the morning in full sun until early afternoon; then transfer to dappled sunlight or bright shade and let them stay out until 9 or 10 at night. Bring plants back indoors.

Day 5/6: Place plants outdoors in full sun and leave them there all day and night.

Day 7: You can now transplant plants in the garden.

Chapter 3

Vegetables Best Direct-Sown

There are several types of veggies that require direct sowing. These include the root crops. If you try to seed a carrot in a container and transplant it in the ground, for instance, it won't grow at all or will become crooked and not form well. Other types of seeds are just easier to grow directly in the garden, like lettuces and other leafy greens.

When you transplant a vegetable plant, it loses time in the growth process as it adjusts to transplanting. This process can take a week or more.

Here are veggies that you generally will want to direct-seed:

Beets	Pumpkins
Carrots	Radishes
Garlic	Rutabagas
Leeks	Shallots
Lettuce (leaf)	Spinach
Onions	Sprouts
Parsnips	Sweet potatoes
Peanuts	Turnips

Seeding Directly into the Garden

Seeding directly into the garden, be it in the ground, a raised bed or container, is an expedient method. Plants that remain where you seed them tend to be healthy and will produce more quickly than transplants. This method is also the only one to use for root crops, which don't transplant well.

To have success direct seeding outdoors, keep a few things in mind:

- Weed the planting area well. Tiny seedlings are no match for water-thirsty weeds.
- Consider seed size. The rule of thumb is to plant seeds the same depth as their length or diameter. That means that tiny seeds are planted at or near the soil surface, while bigger seeds are planted deeper. For instance, tomato seeds only require being planted an 1/8th of an inch deep, while you'll want to plant corn seeds at 1/4 inch deep. Some large seeds like fava beans will go in at 1/2 an inch deep.
- Moisten the planting area before planting. This will help seeds adhere to the soil in which you plant them, and they will have less of a chance of washing away when you first water.

Propagating (AKA Seeding for Vegetables)

- Avoid planting on a windy day.
- To broadcast small seed, put a handful in your palm and sprinkle the seed with the fingertips of your other hand.
- Overseed. When seeding outdoors, your germination rate will be lower than indoors, due to the elements. Compensate for this by planting extra seed.
- Water the planting area well after you finish seeding. Because the seeds haven't yet set down roots and will easily float away, water with a fine spray until the area is well soaked.
- Keep the seeded area moist but not soggy until the seedlings emerge. To help ensure that small seed, such as carrots, stay wet while germinating, cover the planting area with newspaper once you've soaked the soil after seeding. Then soak the newspaper and secure with rocks at the perimeter. Keep the newspaper and soil wet, which will hasten germination and ensure the seeds never dry out. Once the seedlings emerge, remove the newspaper.
- When seedlings emerge, gradually pull back on watering, but don't ever let seedlings go dry. Their small root systems will quickly perish. Pay special attention when the weather is windy and warm.

Sprinkling Carrot Seeds into Raised Bed

Moist Newspaper Secured Over Seeds

Seed Longevity and Storage

Most seed packets come with more seeds than you can possibly plant in one season. When properly stored, most seeds will last for 5 to 7 years. Keep in mind that the older the seed, the less viable it will tend to be. If planting older seed, ensure a better chance of germination by overseeding.

To keep seed viable as long as

Chapter 3

possible, store in a cool, dry location out of direct sunlight. Make sure that the seed stays dry, as moisture can cause the seeds to germinate in the packets.

Seed Harvesting

It's possible to harvest seed from your garden and plant them the following season. Only harvest seed from open-pollinated crops. To do so, let the vegetable mature on the vine. This means, for instance, waiting until a pea pod is brown and crispy, and the peas inside are hard and dry like you'd find them in a seed packet.

Propagating (AKA Seeding for Vegetables)

Chapter 4
Pests (and Diseases)

Pests are an annoying, yet inevitable part of vegetable gardening. After all, you are providing small critters like aphids, and larger invaders like rabbits, with a tasty menu on which to dine. Add to this the fact that Southern California is a veritable paradise for what are known as exotic pests.

Defined by California Department of Food and Agriculture as "organisms that are introduced into an area beyond their natural range," exotic pests can do a great deal of damage in the Southern California garden. Because they are out of their range, they also tend to be away from predators that keep them in check in their native habitats. That results in nonnative species having a "field day" in Southern California gardens.

Of course, it's a bummer to go out into the garden to harvest the fruits of your labor to find they've been gnawed on or eaten altogether. Your first instinct (after stomping your feet) may be to annihilate every bug in the garden. Before you do that, step back and consider the following.

Pests are Just Doing their Jobs

The fact is that pests are a natural part of the plant world. We have many reasons to thank them. Their primary reason for existing is to target dead and dying plant material and return it to the soil in order to feed the soil, including beneficial soil organisms. Insects also serve as an important source of food for wildlife. For instance, birds require hundreds of worms to feed their baby chicks. Without certain insects like flies, we'd be surrounded by dead organic matter of all sorts.

Most Bugs are Good for the Garden

Some insects are destructive and definitely need to be controlled. This is especially the case if you have an invasion of a pest that is decimating your crops. But keep in mind that while some insects are pests and destructive, of the more than 1.5 million known insect species on the planet, more than 97 percent are beneficial for the garden, or simply benign and serving as sources of food for wildlife. That means that less than 3 percent of insects are what would be considered nuisance or agricultural pests.

Attempting to annihilate every bug in your yard is harmful to your garden, your neighborhood, your health, and the planet. It's also an impossible undertaking. It turns out that beneficial insects oftentimes are more delicate than invasive species. So, you can kill everything in sight, and then the invasive species just come back full force, with no beneficial species in sight.

Keep in mind as well that beneficial insects perform the vital function of pollinating the crops that feed us. More than 75 percent of produce crops and flowering plants rely on distribution of pollen by animals, and most of that work is done by insects, including bees, butterflies, moths, beetles, and yes, even flies. Honeybees pollinate $15 billion in crops every year. Some insects such as ladybird beetles and green lacewings even eat "bad" bugs that harm crops.

What about Diseases?

Diseases are another inevitable in the vegetable garden. And they are equally as worrisome. Watching your squash plant leaves turn as white as snow with powdery mildew, for instance, can be distressing. Like pests, diseases are also around to maintain checks and balances in the environment. They also break down plant tissue and send it back to the earth.

What to do about Pests/Diseases?

If you have a few pests here and there, don't be alarmed. As mentioned, pests are a natural part of the garden ecosystem. Aphids on a cauliflower plant will most likely be eaten by green lacewings, ladybird beetles, or birds in short order. And if some leaves get powdery mildew, simply cut them off and dispose of them in a covered trash bin.

Pests (and Diseases)

Planting disease-resistant varieties is also a good way to keep problems at bay. Thanks to hybridization efforts, you can find many disease-resistant vegetable plants today. There are also many heirlooms that are hardy and healthy and have stood the test of time. Look for the term disease-resistant in plant descriptions when purchasing seed or transplants.

Another sign that a plant will be strong and problem-free in your vegetable garden is if it has the All-America Selections (AAS) Winner designation. All-America Selections is a non-profit organization that trials plants to determine garden performance and selects winners each year. Winners offer superior garden performance, including disease-resistance. The 2021 winner in the vegetable category was the hybrid Squash Goldilocks F1.

When things get out of hand in your garden with pests and diseases, though, you may have a cultural problem or nutrient deficiency that needs to be addressed. Pests and diseases don't tend to attack healthy plants. Provide plants with the correct exposure in terms of lighting and the right amount of water and fertilizer, and you give your vegetable plants more than a fighting chance of warding off pests and diseases.

Common Veggie Garden Pests

Familiarizing yourself with common pests you may find in your SoCal garden will help you identify them when they strike. While certain vegetables tend to attract specific pests — for instance cabbage butterfly caterpillars love dining on *Brassica* plants — many are equal opportunity munchers, such as aphids.

Cabbage Butterfly Caterpillar

If any of these pests become invasive, you can use one of the controls shared later in the chapter, depending on the intruder. See table on next page for full list.

Aphids	Leafminers
Bagrada Bugs	Nematodes
Beetles (Cucumber, Colorado potato)	Possums
Birds	Rabbits
Cabbage Root Maggot	Raccoons
Caterpillars (Cabbage Moth/Loopers)	Snails/Slugs
Corn Earworms	Sowbugs
Cutworms	Spider Mites
Gophers	Thrips
Grasshoppers	Tobacco/Tomato Hornworms
Leafhoppers	Whiteflies

Identifying and Managing Insects

If you spot an occasional insect in the garden, remember that it may be a good guy eating up some bad guys. However, if you notice what appears to be an invasion with a lot of insects feasting on plants or veggies, it's a good idea to figure out what you're dealing with and then manage the problem.

Here are the steps to identifying the potential pest:

1. **Observe.** Watch the insect for awhile. Is he busily munching away, causing a lot of damage to the plant? Or is he possibly eating other insects? For instance, he could be a good guy preying on smaller insects that are causing problems. A good tool for observing and identifying what you're seeing is a high powered hand lens, such as a jeweler's loop. This handy device will allow you to see what's going on up close. If your insect visitor is accompanied by a large number of pests just like him, you likely have an infestation.

2. **Research the pest.** Take a photo of the pest and then look the pest up online. The USDA Agricultural Research Service has an image gallery, which you can find here: https://www.ars.usda.gov/oc/images/image-gallery/. You can also look for images on university sites, such as the UC Davis Department of Entomology and Nematology, here: https://entomology.ucdavis.edu/. There are also apps for identifying bugs in the garden, such as the Picture Insect - Bug Identifier.

Note: If after some research you aren't able to identify the pest and it is causing a lot of damage in your garden, contact your local university cooperative extension office, as you may have a new invasive exotic species in your yard.

Garden Pest Solutions

When you find it necessary to cut down on the pest population in your garden, there are a variety of options from which to choose. By using one or more of the following solutions, you will be taking what is known as an Integrated Pest Management (IPM) approach. This is a safety-first approach originally developed for commercial agriculture that is also ideal for the home garden. The primary aim of this method is to prevent problems in the first place by proper planting and maintenance of plants. When problems arise, you try the least harmful and disruptive methods first.

Barrier Methods

Keeping pests away from crops is sometimes an option:

- Copper stripping designed for gardens. The stripping is placed around plant pots and in other strategic areas where pests climb up and onto plants. Copper works especially well for crawling insects, such as slugs and snails, which are zapped when they try to cross over the material.
- Floating row cover or netting. These items block pests like birds and possums from being able to easily get to crops. The goal is to make it inconvenient enough that they move on.
- Screened in barrier/fencing. This will keep out smaller pests, such as grasshoppers and cabbage butterflies and their caterpillars, as well as unwanted larger pests, such as rabbits, raccoons, possums, birds, and deer.
- Plant collars. Placing a collar around vegetable seedlings will protect the plants from being eaten by pests such as cutworms. Make a collar from a small plastic food container. Cut the bottom out of the container and place it over the plant, pushing the container 1/2 inch into the soil.
- Underground cages and barriers. This is often the only way to keep digging pests like gophers from eating root crops and destroying the root system of other plants.

Physical Controls
Some effective ways to control pests that are nontoxic include:
- Spraying with a strong spray of water. Use this method for fragile, small insect pests like aphids.
- Handpicking. This works best with large pests that you can easily locate and handle, such as caterpillars, snails, and slugs.
- Pruning. You may find a portion of a vegetable plant that is completely infested. Prune it off and throw away in a covered trash can.
- Trap. You can trap pests in a couple of ways. Yellow, white or red sticky traps are very sticky pieces of thin cardboard that attract certain pests that then get stuck on them and die. Pheromones are chemicals that allow for communication between insects of the same species. You'll find sticky pheromone traps that also lure insects, which then get stuck and perish.
- Elevate plants and vegetables. Keeping stems and developing produce off the soil helps to keep the plant safe from crawling insects such as sowbugs. Additionally, it will prevent contact with microscopic bacteria in soil that will eat ripening vegetables.
- Apply pine needles. Pine needles are naturally serrated. That means that pests like snails and slugs get cut when trying to walk over the needles. Apply pine needles at the base of plants to prevent intruders. The needles will also keep hanging vegetables from touching soil.

Interplant with Herbs and Marigolds

Sometimes called companion planting, interplanting your vegetable garden with certain herbs and marigolds can prevent insects from feeding. Some good herbs for interplanting that are strong smelling and fend off pests include basil, rosemary, French tarragon, lavender, and garlic chives.

Marigolds are especially effective at deterring pests such as aphids and various beetles, and snails. They release an oil that coats surrounding plants that pests don't like. Below ground, they deter and kill destructive nematodes by excreting a chemical that kills them. When the marigolds are finished growing, till them into the soil for even more effective pest control.

Pests (and Diseases)

Marigolds in Veggie Garden

Use Biological Pest Control

You can get some vegetable pests to a tolerable level by taking a page from Mother Nature. Biological controls are living organisms, such as beneficial insects. They fall into two main categories. These are beneficial predators and parasites.

One of the most common beneficial predator insects is the ladybug. This cute, little bug and its larvae, which resemble an alligator with black and orange spots, devour soft-bodied troublemakers like aphids. You can also find praying mantis and green lacewings to serve the same purpose.

Ladybug Eating Aphids

Rotate Crops

Planting the same crop in the same area each season will result in the same pests (and diseases) reappearing. Rotate where you plant crops each time you plant. If gardening space is limited, instead of rotating the crops, mix things up by replacing the soil in the ground with soil from another area of the yard. When growing in containers and raised beds, move soil around or replace with new soil.

Beneficial parasites don't consume the entire pest, but instead take up residence in the bodies of insect pests and feed off their innards. Many are

Chapter 4

parasitic wasps that lay eggs inside of their hosts. When the wasps hatch, they begin consuming the host. You can see the effects of this process in your garden with a high powered hand lens. Look for insect carcasses attached to stems and leaves that appear dry and hollowed out. If you find these in your garden, it means that beneficial parasites are at work for you!

While nematodes are often thought of as "bad", because some varieties do cause harm by eating plant roots, there are beneficial nematodes that will feed on their harmful counterparts as well as other underground pests, like the larvae of fungus gnats.

Some organic fertilizers do double duty by providing pest control. For instance, adding worm castings (worm poop) to your soil has been shown to suppress a wide range of plant pests. This has to do with the fact that worm castings contain chitinase, an enzyme that breaks down the exoskeletons of many insects. When the level of chitinase becomes high in soil, insect pests will even leave the area.

Another organic fertilizer that provides micronutrients to the soil is micronized rock dust. This also clogs the breathing slits of many insect pests, including aphids and mites. Simply dust the micronized rock dust on top of the plants or insects.

Organic Pesticides

Using organic pesticides may be necessary when you can't get an infestation under control with gentler means. Here are some solutions. Keep in mind that pesticides will kill off beneficial as well as harmful insects. And just because they are organic, doesn't mean they can't harm you. Always follow package directions when using any organic pesticide. Use the following products judiciously, and as little as possible.

Bacillus thuringiensis (BT): This is a naturally occurring bacterium that kills larvae. It is effective against caterpillars, including tomato hornworms, and the larvae of mosquitoes, Colorado potato beetles, and cabbage worms. Keep in mind that it will kill all butterfly and moth caterpillars that it comes in contact with.

Pests (and Diseases)

Diatomaceous Earth (DE): This powdery substance consists of the skeletons of microscopic marine organisms. DE matts up on insects, damaging their protective coats. DE can be used to combat aphids, cutworms, slugs, snails, and ants. (Ants are a problem in the vegetable garden, as they protect and herd aphids. They do this so they can consume the honeydew that aphids excrete when feeding on your vegetable plants).

Ultra-Fine Horticultural Oils

Oils for the garden are designed to suffocate a wide variety of pests and their eggs. They will also smother disease spores, including funguses. Use horticultural oils to kill aphids, thrips, and whiteflies. Avoid spraying when there are vegetables on the plant. (To prevent corn earworms, apply 20 drops of mineral oil onto each silk when they appear).

Isopropyl Alcohol

Soft-bodied pests such as aphids will dry and shrivel up if sprayed or dabbed with rubbing alcohol. The alcohol penetrates and damages their protective coatings.

Neem Oil

The active ingredient in this organic pest control is azadirachtin, pressed from the seed of the neem tree *Azadirachta indica*. Neem oil is an effective insecticide, fungicide, and miticide. It is an appetite suppressant that make insects less likely to feed on plants. The substance also inhibits insect mating and reduces female fertility. Neem oil should be diluted: 1/2 tsp neem oil per 16 oz of warm distilled water and 1/2 Tbsp of pure Castile soap. (For an even more potent solution, add 10 drops of citronella essential oil to every 16 oz of prepared neem oil.)

Insecticidal Soap Sprays

You'll find products on the market designed to suffocate pests that are made of soap, vegetable fatty acids, and sticking and spreading agents. There are many recipes to make your own soap spray with dish soap, but they don't have spreading and sticking agents. That means as soon as the pest moves, the bond is broken, and the pest can breathe and escape. Many commercial soap sprays have additional organic pesticides, such as neem or pyrethrins.

Chapter 4

Pyrethrins

This insecticide is a strong but effective method of destroying unwanted pests. Derived from the dried flowers of the pyrethrum daisy, the substance will kill a wide variety of pests, including grasshoppers. Keep in mind that products containing pyrethrins will also kill beneficial insects. The insecticide does break down quickly in sunlight, so there are no residual effects.

Spinosad

Composed of a naturally occurring soil bacterium, Spinosad can be toxic to a variety of pests, including leafminers, thrips, spider mites, ants, and mosquitoes. It has been registered for use as a pesticide with the EPA since 1997 and some of the products in which Spinosad appears are registered for organic agriculture. When insect pests eat or touch Spinosad, it causes uncontrollable muscle spasms. This leads to paralysis and death within 1 to 2 days. Spinosad breaks down rapidly in sunlight, so there are no residual effects.

Sulfur Dust

An essential soil nutrient that lowers soil pH, sulfur dust also kills thrips and spider mites.

Slug and Snail Bait

Use Sluggo brand, which won't harm animals that might eat the bait. The active ingredient is iron phosphate, which degrades and becomes a part of the soil if not consumed by snails and slugs.

To Note: When buying insecticides and fungicides, look for OMRI certification on the label, indicating the product is used for organic production.

Common Veggie Garden Diseases

Take a look at the list of potential vegetable garden diseases, and you might be scared off from starting a veggie garden. Keep in mind that these are potential diseases. If you keep your plants as healthy as possible and grow disease-resistant varieties, you generally won't have trouble with these problems. The key is to remember that certain plants are susceptible to certain diseases. By heeding the ideal growing conditions for plants, they won't generally succumb to disease.

Pests (and Diseases)

Septoria Fungal Leaf Spot on Tomato Plant Leaves

In general, fungal diseases, including rots, wilts, spotting and mildew, start with overwatering or conditions that are too moist. Your best bet for preventing these diseases from occurring in the first place is to avoid overwatering and wetting foliage, plant in well-draining soil, provide plants with the ideal sun exposure, and plant in an area that has good air-circulation.

Some organic solutions for diseases include *Bacillus amyloliquefaciens*, a bacterium that works as a fungicide and a bactericide. Sulfur dust is also an effective fungicide.

Leafhoppers suck plant sap from leaves, causing extensive damage

Viruses tend to be spread by certain pests, such as leafhoppers. Once a plant has a virus, it's often impossible to get rid of it, although the plant may continue to grow, anyway. This is where rotating crops becomes mission critical. If you have a crop that succumbs to a virus or disease, it's important to not plant the same family of plants in that area for at least 4 years. If space is limited, you can dig out the soil in the planting area and replace with soil from another area of the garden. With pots and raised beds, if you have a problem with a virus, exchange soil or replace it.

Symptoms for the following diseases vary, but generally when a plant is affected you'll see wilting, black spots, curling, and overall loss of health and vitality.

Angular Leaf Spot	Fusarium Root Rot
Asters Yellows	Fusarium Wilt
Bacterial Leaf Spot	Gray Mold
Blight	Leaf Blight
Blossom End Rot	Mosaic Virus
Botrytis Fungus	Pink Root
Club Root	Powdery Mildew
Curly Dwarf Virus/ Curly Top Virus	Purple Blotch
Crown Rot	Root Rot
Damping Off	Spotted Wilt Virus
Downy Mildew	Sudden Wilt
Fungal Leaf Spot	Verticillium Wilt

Chapter 4

Pests (and Diseases)

Chapter 5
Growing Lifelong Gardeners (Gardening with Kids)

Growing and harvesting delicious veggies is quite a rush for an adult. Multiply that feeling one-thousand fold, and you'll feel how exciting the experience is for little tykes. Introduce a child to gardening, and that makes the experience thrilling for everyone involved.

Children are natural gardeners. With their extensive imaginations and unending curiosity, they love planting seeds, watching them sprout and grow, and eating the results. They also enjoy nurturing plants. Research shows that nature stimulates children's senses, and that promotes exploration.

There is always something happening in the vegetable garden. Leaves sway in the breeze, birds fly overhead, and colorful bugs crawl on plants. With their short statures that offer a unique vantage point, children see garden activity that adults often don't. Is that a worm in the soil? A bee in a mud puddle? An ant crawling at the base of a vegetable plant? The adventures are truly endless.

Gardening with kids can also spark an adult's interest in gardening and the satisfaction of growing your own produce. Feeling the joy of your child or grandchild digging in the dirt can motivate you to plant the garden paradise you've been dreaming about for years. Kids will also help ensure that you keep planting and planning your garden. You don't want to disappoint a little one expecting to harvest and snack on yummy veggies like cucamelons!

Green "Computer Labs"

Gardening teaches kids a wide variety of life lessons in a fun way that doesn't seem like learning at all. In the process of planting, nurturing, and harvesting, children learn skills and coping mechanisms that give them the necessary resilience and adaptability that life demands.

Even better, gardening is an antidote to the structured, high-tech world in which youngsters find themselves. Most kid's lives are filled with organized sports and activities and play dates. Digging, planting, and munching from the garden gives children a breath of fresh air in more ways than one. The sensory aspects of gardening ignite imaginations and power creativity. Kids of all ages enjoy gardening — tykes, tweens, and teens.

Patience

Gardening is an antidote to our instant gratification society. Waiting for seeds to germinate and plants to produce edible produce takes time. As they watch and wait, children learn that you can't rush processes or people. Mother Nature takes her own sweet time, but the wait is well worth it. Children come to understand that gardening, like life, is a process. Given time, the garden will reward them, and there are always surprises to look forward to along the way.

Patiently waiting 5 months for our first carrot harvest

Stick-to-itiveness

Children who garden soon see that plants don't give up easily. A windstorm can whip through and tear up leaves and dry up soil, or a rainstorm can flood the backyard, but the vegetable garden will still be standing once the dust settles or the

Growing Lifelong Gardeners

storm clouds cease. Letting kids experiment in the garden gives them a sense of empowerment over their lives that results in them realizing that if they stick to their goals, they can succeed.

Compassion

Through gardening, children take responsibility for another life. Once children have lovingly cared for pumpkin plants, it's hard for them to do anything that might harm the earth. Nature also provides a compassionate way to learn about life cycles. Plants grow, bud, and produce vegetables, then die, and their seed can be saved for future plants.

Skills and Information

Research has found that children need more than traditional outdoor play equipment to develop and become lifelong learners. Gardening provides an outdoor laboratory that can be used to teach just about any subject. So effective are green classrooms that schools across the nation now use gardens as a teaching tool. Lessons taught in classrooms can be reinforced and enhanced within the school garden setting. Some schools that have initiated participatory school gardens have found that science and math scores rise.

By taking on the responsibility of caring for plants and maintaining compost piles and worm bins, kids learn lessons in science and math. You can also use the garden to teach kids about colors, the alphabet, seasons, counting, and where food originates. Opportunities are also ripe for learning about history and social studies through lessons about indigenous plants and how people have used those plants over the years as food and medicine. Insects, which abound in a healthy garden, also give many opportunities to teach about biology and entomology. And then there are the many botany lessons always taking place in the garden, including about processes like photosynthesis.

Good Nutrition & Healthy Habits

When children grow their own produce, they tend to gobble it up. This often occurs right there in the garden,

Chapter 5

so have a hose ready to rinse off the produce! There's something about the ownership kids feel in having a hand in growing vegetables that motivates them to enjoy the fruits of their labor. You'll find they suddenly devour vegetables they may have turned their noses up to at the dinner table. Through the love of produce that ensues from gardening, children come to learn that what they choose to put in their mouths has a profound effect on their health.

Proud of his sugar snap pea harvest, Noah ate them all in one sitting.

Stewardship

We want to pass our planet on to young people in tune with the earth and respectful of Mother Nature's cycles. Nurturing a vegetable garden teaches children to look outside of themselves. Gardening provides a sense of empowerment and ownership of the planet. Kids learn by gardening about sustainability, including composting, water conservation, and gardening organically.

Sowing the Seeds for a Love of Gardening

Gardening with children can start with a small container with just one veggie plant. The key is to give kids something of their own to plant, cultivate, and nurture. Here are some tips for teaching children a love of gardening they'll carry into adulthood.

Begin anytime. Kids can start as early as 18 months in the garden, although they'll be more adept at planting and begin to understand what they're doing starting at about age 3. Have children work alongside you in the garden

Growing Lifelong Gardeners

during the early stages, then graduate to giving them their own containers and plots.

Keep it simple. You might have a vision of a large, farmlike garden plot, but it's best to start small and work your way up to more elaborate gardening plans. Keep in mind, too, that young children don't have long attention spans. Start with containers or a section of raised bed or ground soil.

Try fast starter crops. Beginning with crops that sprout and bear quickly is a good idea — especially for really young gardeners. Good starter crops include sprouts, radishes, green beans, peas, and squash.

Let them explore and experiment. Allowing children to grow what they want and care for the plants in the manner they wish to teaches many useful lessons. They'll learn by trial and error, and hands on learning is often the best teacher.

Make it fun. Remember that the whole goal of gardening is to enjoy yourself just like your young gardener. Get down in the dirt with your little one to watch an ant walk across the grass. Seeing things from a child's perspective will make the experience memorable for everyone.

Happy Harvest Time

Chapter 6:
Vegetables to Grow in your SoCal Garden

You'll find a plethora of options when it comes to the vegetables you can grow in your SoCal garden. With our mild, Mediterranean climate, most types of veggies thrive. The more than 38 vegetables on the following pages give you plenty of options for growing an abundant, delicious harvest.

Organized in alphabetical order, you'll find all of the favorites, as well as some lesser known veggies that deserve wider appreciation. Each vegetable section gives specific growing advice. Discover what kind of soil each veggie likes and how to prepare the planting area. Where to plant, how to water, and fertilizing are also covered, as well as diseases to look out for. Use the secret growing tips to enhance your veggie gardening experience. Also learn about the nutrition packed into each veggie, and savor recipes from your harvest.

If the myriad of choices for vegetable gardening are a little overwhelming for you, start small. Choose two or three types of veggies that you and your family like eating, and begin with those. When making your selections, pay careful attention to the lighting requirements. If a vegetable plant requires full sun, it won't do well in a shaded area of your yard. Also consider how much space is required for growing each vegetable. For the best results, choose crops you have room to grow. If growing space is limited, containers are a good option. Each vegetable section indicates if the veggie is a container growing candidate. Many vegetable varieties thrive in pots on patios and balconies.

Artichokes

Though they feature a prickly exterior, what hides at the heart of an artichoke is tender and tasty. A member of the thistle family, this popular vegetable grows well in SoCal, especially along the coast. The edible part of the artichoke is an unopened flower bud.

Artichoke plants reach 4-feet tall and 6- to 8-feet wide. If you can dedicate the space, they will grow as a perennial in SoCal, producing every year for you. However, if planting room is limited, you can also grow them as an annual.

In addition to offering you a delish eating experience, artichoke plants decorate the landscape. Native to the Mediterranean, the artichoke grows into a silvery-green, fountain-like plant that makes an architectural statement. Unharvested buds open to reveal eye-catching, bristly, purple flower heads. They can be cut and dried and used in floral arrangements.

Nutritional Nugget:
Artichokes are loaded with nutrients, especially folate and vitamins C and K, along with minerals such as magnesium, phosphorus, and potassium. Another fun fact — a phytochemical in artichokes, cynarin, inhibits the sweet taste receptor on your tongue so that food/drink eaten afterward tastes sweeter temporarily.

Growing Tips

Growing Season:
Fall - Early Summer
(Year-Round along Coast)

Container Growing Candidate:
No. (When grown in containers, artichokes tend to be small).

Location:
Full sun in a spot that gets afternoon shade during summer if inland. Ensure there is ample growing room.

Soil:
Rich, well-draining soil. If planting in the ground, mix into the top 8 to 12 inches of clay soil a 3- to 4-inch layer of compost and 1 to 2 cups of pumice. Bulk up sandy soil with a 4- to 5-inch layer of compost.

Planting:
Well-worked ground soil or raised bed is best. Plant October through March. You'll find bare-root artichokes in late fall and early winter, and transplants from fall through spring. Plant 4 to 6 feet apart. Ensure that the crown, which is the green upper part of the plant that connects to the roots, isn't below the soil. If you bury the crown, the plant may succumb to crown rot. Water well after planting.

Fertilizing:
Fertilize at planting time with an organic, well-balanced, dry vegetable fertilizer. Once the plant is growing, feed spring, summer, and fall with an organic, well-balanced, liquid fertilizer.

Watering:
Artichokes require constant moisture and don't do well when the ground dries out. Water young plants daily to keep the soil moist but not soggy. Once the plants grow new leaves after planting, water 2 to 4 times a week, depending on weather. Conserve moisture by mulching. Place mulch 2 to 3 inches away from the base of the plant. Don't water in winter when the plant goes dormant.

Diseases:
Curly Dwarf Virus. **Prevention/Solution**: Remove and destroy infected plants. Weed out milk thistle, which also hosts the disease.
Botrytis Fungus. **Solution:** Remove and destroy infected plant parts. (Common in rainy, humid weather).
Crown Rot. **Prevention:** Keep the area around the crown dry; avoid letting soil pile up around the crown.

Secret Growing Tip:
Artichokes grow side shoots, also known as suckers, in the ground around the base of plants. These will become whole new plants. To avoid crowded conditions, break them off when they appear and root them in another area of the garden or in containers. Keep the side shoots shaded until they root.

Harvesting:
Artichoke plants will produce a dozen or more buds spring through early summer, with one central bud on the main stalk and smaller buds on side stalks. Harvest when buds are still plump and tight. Use pruners to cut the heads off, including stalk, just above a set of leaves. Flush out insects hidden in the artichoke by soaking in a bowl of water with 2 tsp salt and 2 tsp vinegar.

Arugula

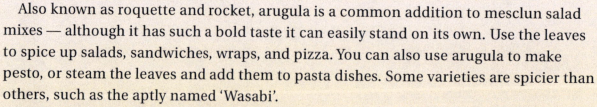

Of all greens to grow in the garden, arugula has one of the most distinctive flavors. Pick arugula homegrown, and you'll be surprised at how much more flavorful this peppery green is compared to store-bought.

Also known as roquette and rocket, arugula is a common addition to mesclun salad mixes — although it has such a bold taste it can easily stand on its own. Use the leaves to spice up salads, sandwiches, wraps, and pizza. You can also use arugula to make pesto, or steam the leaves and add them to pasta dishes. Some varieties are spicier than others, such as the aptly named 'Wasabi'.

While arugula can be grown during SoCal warm months, it thrives at cooler times of the year. Hot days tend to cause arugula to bolt (go to seed). When this happens, the leaves become bitter and rough in texture, and then the plant slows down growth and dies back.

If arugula finishes its life cycle without any interruption from warm weather, it will eventually shoot up to 3 feet tall and go to seed. You can continue to eat the small side shoots for several weeks after this occurs. The plant will reseed itself in surrounding soil, creating whole new plants.

Tomato & Arugula Salad

2 large or 4 medium tomatoes, cut into 1-inch chunks
4 cups of arugula, rinsed and torn
1 tablespoon of capers
1 small clove of garlic, crushed
1 teaspoon of olive oil
1/2 tablespoon of fresh squeezed lemon juice
Cracked pepper and sea salt to taste

Combine all ingredients and enjoy!

Nutritional Nugget:

Arugula is a nutrient-dense food high in fiber and phytochemicals, including glucosinolates. In addition to giving arugula its distinctive spicy taste and strong scent, studies also show that glucosinolates may fight damage to our body's cells.

Growing Tips

Growing Season:
Fall - Spring
(Year-Round along Coast)

Container Growing Candidate:
Yes. Minimum 5-gallon container.

Location:
Full sun to light shade. Well-worked ground soil, container or raised bed.

Soil:
Rich, well-draining soil. Mix into the top 6 inches of clay soil a 2- to 3-inch layer of compost, if planting in the ground. Keep the growing area weed free.

Planting:
Plant seeds directly in the garden or in containers and transplant when arugula is 3 inches tall. You can also find arugula transplants at the nursery. If seeding in the ground, sprinkle seeds over the soil as evenly as possible, then cover the seeds with a 1/8- to 1/4-inch layer of lightweight potting soil or seed starting mix. Water well with a fine mist. The seeds take 7 to 12 days to germinate. Keep the soil surface moist during germination. Thin seedlings to 4 to 5 inches apart when they reach 3 inches tall.

Fertilizing:
Fertilize at planting time with an organic, well-balanced, dry vegetable fertilizer. Arugula grows as a weed in the Mediterranean, so it doesn't need any more fertilizing after that. Feed arugula plants that seeded themselves once the leaves reach 4 inches tall, using an organic, well-balanced, liquid fertilizer.

Watering:
Water young arugula plants when the soil surface is approaching dryness. Once arugula reaches 4 inches tall, you can wait until the top 1/2 inch of soil has dried before watering.

Diseases:
Bacterial Leaf Spot, Downy Mildew. **Prevention:** Immediately remove and dispose of infected plants. Rotate crops. Don't overcrowd plants.

Harvesting:
30 to 45 days after planting. Pinch or cut leaves off at the base of the plant, or in the case of a large plant, next to the main stem.

Secret Cooking Tip:
Arugula flowers, which come in yellow and white, can also be eaten. They add even more zing to a salad — and some color.

Self-Seeded Arugula

Asparagus

Though asparagus takes 2 to 3 years to produce a full crop, it's worth the wait. Prepare the planting bed well, and you'll be rewarded each spring for 15+ years with plenty of tasty asparagus to savor. Once the initial planting is done, you need only keep the asparagus well watered and supplied with nutrients.

While asparagus can be grown from seed, doing so means you must wait an extra year before harvesting a crop. For that reason, many gardeners choose to speed up the process by planting 1-year-old crowns. This leads to harvesting a few spears the second year, and a full crop by the third year.

Asparagus comes in what are known as traditional and all male varieties. One variety especially suited to SoCal is the male variety 'UC 157', developed by the University of California. Male varieties produce larger and more spears, because they don't dedicate energy to creating seeds. Such varieties are also resistant to diseases that affect asparagus, such as Fusarium wilt.

Nutritional Nugget:
Asparagus contains high levels of fiber and the amino acid asparagine, making it a natural diuretic that helps you beat bloat. The vegetable is also full of folate and vitamins A, C, E, and K.

Growing Tips

Growing Season:
Fall - Spring

Container Growing Candidate:
No.

Location:
Full sun in an area protected from winds. The planting area must be weed free. Invasive grass species like Bermuda will choke out asparagus plants. Consider planting in a raised bed where weeds are fewer and easier to remove and good drainage is guaranteed.

Soil:
Rich, well-draining soil. (See "planting" for soil preparation).

Planting:
Plant fall through early spring. To prepare a new bed for planting, dig out a 1-foot deep by 1-foot wide trench long enough to accommodate planting each asparagus 12 to 18 inches apart from one another. If creating more than one trench, space them 3 feet apart. When planting in clay soil, prior to digging the trench, mix into the soil a 4- to 5-inch layer of compost. After the trench is created, fill with 4 inches of bagged chicken manure. Sprinkle on top of that a half cup of bonemeal for each linear foot of trench. Soak the bottom of the trench with water. Cover the bonemeal with 3 inches of soil, then mound up the soil along the length of the trench. Place the asparagus plants on the mound every 12 to 18 inches, letting their roots hang over the side. Then cover the plant roots with soil until the plants are 1 inch below the soil surface. Water well. As the plants grow, gradually add more soil until the trench is filled to the same level as surrounding soil. Don't cover any growing asparagus tips while doing so.

Fertilizing:
Except for the first year of planting, apply an organic, high-nitrogen fertilizer such as blood meal or feather meal in early spring before spears emerge and again when the harvest finishes. You can use a liquid fertilizer, or dig a small trench along one side of the planting bed and add dry fertilizer. Cover with soil and water thoroughly. Additionally, mulch with compost every February.

Watering:
For the first year of growth, keep the asparagus bed well watered. Thereafter, water when the weather is dry and the top 2 inches of soil have dried out.

Diseases:
Fusarium Wilt. **Prevention/Solution**: Caused by fungus in the soil. Remove and destroy infected plants. Weed out milk thistle, which also hosts the disease.
Botrytis Fungus. **Solution:** Remove and destroy infected plant parts. (Common in rainy, humid weather).
Crown Rot. **Prevention:** Keep the area around the crown dry and avoid letting soil pile up next to it.

Secret Growing Tip:
When plants turn brown in late fall or early winter, cut them to the ground, unless in an area of SoCal that experiences frosty nights regularly. In that case, leave the plants until spring, which will protect the crowns.

Harvesting:
Refrain from harvesting spears the first spring after planting. You want the asparagus plants to create large root masses. The second year after planting you can harvest some spears by snapping or cutting them off at soil-level. Do so for 4 to 6 weeks until new spears appear spindlier than earlier in the season. Then allow the plants to leaf out and grow. This allows for building up reserves for a full crop the next season. The third year after planting, the crop will be much fuller, and you can harvest the entire season, from spring to summer.

Beans

The mainstay of the summer garden, beans are easy to grow and quick to produce. One of the most difficult tasks is deciding which type you'd like to try. The good news is beans don't take up much space in the garden. If you can't decide on one type, try several varieties and enjoy a delicious, abundant crop!

There are two main categories of beans — pole and bush. Pole beans have a climbing habit and require support to grow well. Bush beans are compact plants reaching 1 to 2 feet tall, depending on variety. Bush beans tend to bear earlier in the season, while pole beans are more prolific.

Within these two broad categories, you'll find many bean options, including snap beans, wax beans, shelling beans, filet beans, and dry beans. Snap beans, also known as green beans, come in green, yellow, and purple varieties. They are eaten pod and all when they are young and have some "snap" to them. Wax beans are varieties of snap beans with a shiny coating.

The term string beans, which is the same as snap beans, comes from older varieties that tended to be more stringy than newer hybrids. Filet beans are widely grown in France, where they are known as *haricots verts*. They are a type of bush snap bean that you harvest at peak flavor when the bean is just 1/8- to 1/4-inch in diameter. With shelling and dry beans you harvest the beans from the shells and cook and eat them.

Other Bean Varieties:

In addition to snap beans, it's possible to grow a few other beans in the SoCal garden. These include lima beans, fava beans (grow in cool weather), and runner beans. The latter bean is categorized as dry, meaning that it is cooked for consumption once the pod matures and dries on the vine. The Scarlet Runner Bean variety produces eye-catching orange-red flowers that become bean pods.

Growing Tips

Growing Season:
Spring - Late Summer

Container Growing Candidate:
Yes. Minimum 10-gallon container.

Location:
Full sun. In the ground, raised bed or container.

Soil:
Rich, well-draining, loose soil. Mix into the top 8 to 10 inches of soil a 4- to 5-inch layer of compost. If the soil is particularly compacted, add pumice to improve drainage.

Planting:
Sow bean seeds directly into the ground, into a raised bed or container, or plant transplants. Plant bean seeds with the scar side down 1 inch deep. Space bush beans 1 to 2 feet apart. For pole beans, provide support before planting. This can be a teepee that you create by arranging three to four 8-foot tall bamboo or green garden poles and tying at the top. Or you can grow beans along other structures, such as walls, fences, and trellises. Plant three to four pole bean seeds around each pole or every 3 inches along other structures. Plant transplants the same distance apart. Bean plants need some initial help winding their way up trellises and poles. Once you get them started, they usually continue on their own.

Fertilizing:
Fertilize at planting time with an organic, well-balanced, dry vegetable fertilizer. Beans are light feeders, so that is all the feeding they need each season.

Watering:
Soak the planting area after planting bean seeds, and then stop until seedlings emerge. Too much water during the germination phase can rot the seeds. Keep seedlings and transplants well watered, especially when beans begin to flower and form pods.

Diseases:
Damping-Off. **Prevention**: Avoid planting in cold, wet soil. Wait until the weather and ground warms. Fusarium Root Rot. **Prevention/Solution:** Destroy infected plants. Plant in well-draining soil. Rotate crops.

Secret Growing Tip:
Beans are legumes, like peas. Both types of plants house nitrogen-fixing bacteria in their roots. That means growing beans enriches your garden soil. Other crops you plant in the area afterward will greatly benefit.

Harvesting:
50 to 70 days, depending on if you planted from seed and the variety. Harvest when the bean pods are young and tender and 3- to 4-inches long. Cut or snap the beans off the plant, being careful not to yank when you do so. The more often you pick the beans, the more the plant will produce, so harvest regularly. If bean pods mature, the plant will stop bearing.

Nutritional Nugget:
Green beans are a good source of fiber, folate, vitamins C and K, and the mineral silicon, which is important for healthy bones, skin, and hair. While green beans are one of the few types of beans that can be eaten raw, as they have a lower lectin content, cooking neutralizes their lectins and improves their taste, digestibility, and antioxidant content.

Beets

The canned beets you may have eaten as a kid pale in comparison to fresh, tasty beets plucked out of the garden bed. With their multitude of shapes, sizes, and colors, beets offer a plethora of delicious options for the home garden.

There are standard bright red beets and candy cane striped beets in white and red. You'll also find orange and yellow beets, and even white ones. While there are many round beets, some are long and cylindrical.

Even better, you can eat the whole beet. The greens make a tasty addition to stir-fries, and when the leaves are young and tender, add a delectable taste to salads.

Beets are a cool-season plant that thrives in SoCal's cool winter days and nights. As a root crop, they require direct seeding into the garden, like the planting of carrots.

Candy Cane Beets

Nutritional Nugget: Beets are a powerhouse of antioxidants, mainly betalains, which support liver function and reduce inflammation. Beet leaves are rich in vitamin K, copper, manganese, and iron.

Growing Tips

Growing Season:
Fall - Winter
(Year-Round along Coast)

Location:
Full sun (minimum 6 hours). Container or raised bed is best.

Container Growing Candidate:
Yes. Minimum 10-gallon container.

Soil:
Rich, well-draining soil. If planting in the ground, loosen clay soil with compost and bulk up sandy soil with compost. Ensure that the ground is free of any impediments, such as stones and sticks. Keep the growing area weed free.

Planting:
Plant seeds 1 inch apart. Then cover the seeds with a 1/8-inch layer of lightweight potting soil or seed starting mix. Water well with a fine mist of water. Cover the area with newspaper or burlap and soak the covering. The seeds take 2 to 3 weeks to germinate. During that time, keep the covering and soil surface moist. Once the tiny seedlings emerge, take off the covering. When seedlings are 3 inches tall, thin to 2 inches apart. Thinning is important, as crowded beets tend to be small and misshapen.

Fertilizing:
Fertilize at planting time with an organic, well-balanced, dry vegetable fertilizer. When plants reach 3- to 4-inches tall, water with an organic, well-balanced, liquid fertilizer every 3 to 4 weeks.

Watering:
Water young plants when the soil surface is approaching dryness. If you wait until the soil surface is dry to touch, you may lose young plants, which have tiny root systems. Avoid allowing tender young beet tops to dry out in Santa Ana winds or on an unseasonably warm day. Once beet tops reach 3 inches tall, begin watering when the soil surface has dried. Lack of water can cause woody, cracked beets, and fluctuations in water can cause splitting.

Diseases:
Cercospora Leaf Spot. **Solution**: Pick off and destroy infected leaves.
Curly Top Virus. **Prevention:** Spread by beet leafhoppers that thrive in weeds — so control weeds.

Secret Growing Tip:
Each beet seed will grow as many as four beets at once. So, even if you are careful to plant seeds 1 inch apart, you are likely to get multiple plants from each seed. Thin to one plant every 2 inches with shears, reserving the largest plants. For best germination, soak beet seeds overnight prior to planting.

Harvesting:
45 to 75 days after planting. You can harvest beets at any size, but small to golf-ball sized are the tastiest. Avoid allowing beets to grow larger than 3 inches in diameter, as they will become woody in texture and lose flavor.

Broccoli

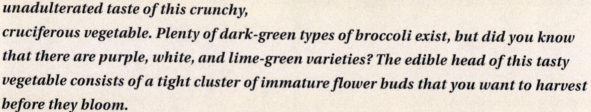

Cut a head of broccoli out of the garden and enjoy the pure, unadulterated taste of this crunchy, cruciferous vegetable. Plenty of dark-green types of broccoli exist, but did you know that there are purple, white, and lime-green varieties? The edible head of this tasty vegetable consists of a tight cluster of immature flower buds that you want to harvest before they bloom.

A member of the *Brassica* family, which includes cabbage, cauliflower, kale, and Brussels sprouts, Broccoli is a cool-season plant. If the weather remains chilly, the plant will thrive. Trouble comes calling when SoCal experiences hot, drying Santa Ana winds, or a hot spell. Then broccoli can bolt, which refers to the head prematurely flowering. At that point, the broccoli needs to be harvested, because when the flowers in the head bloom, the taste is negatively affected.

Broccolini / Broccoli Rabe:

While broccolini may look like immature broccoli, it's a cross created in the early 1990s between broccoli and Chinese broccoli. The latter veggie is leafier than standard broccoli. With broccolini, you get smaller florets of broccoli on longer, leafier stems. This vegetable has a mellower, sweeter flavor than standard broccoli. The long stems also have a nice crunch and offer a good mix of leafy greens. Broccoli rabe is an Italian relative of the standard broccoli. It has a slightly stronger flavor. Grow broccolini and broccoli rabe the same as broccoli, although harvesting times are a little shorter at 50 to 90 days.

Growing Tips

Growing Season:
Fall - Early Spring

Container Growing Candidate:
Yes. Minimum 10-gallon container for one plant.

Location:
Full sun (minimum 6-8 hours).

Soil:
Rich, well-draining soil. Mix into the top 6 to 8 inches of clay soil a 2- to 3-inch layer of compost, if planting in the ground. Ensure the planting area is weed free.

Planting:
Plant 15 to 24 inches apart. For best results, plant transplants from the nursery, or grow from seed in containers and transplant when the plants are 3 inches tall. After heat has passed in fall, plant through midwinter. Broccoli plant stems tend to be crooked toward the base of the plant and fragile. Remove the bottom sets of leaves and plant to cover the crook. This will ensure that the plant stands up straight and grows strong.

Fertilizing:
Fertilize at planting time with an organic, well-balanced, dry vegetable fertilizer. When plants reach 3- to 4-inches tall, water with an organic, well-balanced, liquid fertilizer every 3 to 4 weeks.

Watering:
Keep the soil around young broccoli plants moist but not soggy. Water mature broccoli plants when the top inch of soil has dried out. Do a deep soak when watering.

Diseases:
Downy Mildew, Bacterial Soft Rot. **Prevention:** Plant disease-resistant varieties. Provide good air circulation. Plant in well-draining soil. Rotate crops.

Secret Growing Tip:
One plant can produce broccoli for up to three months thanks to smaller heads that form on secondary (axillary) shoots.

Harvesting:
50 to 110 days after planting. Times vary according to if you grew from seed. With a sharp knife, cut out the central head of the broccoli before it begins to flower. Include stalk when cutting, as this is also edible. If you leave the plant to continue growing, side branches will produce smaller heads that can be harvested.

Nutritional Nugget:
One cup of broccoli has as much vitamin C as an orange! It also boasts more protein than most other vegetables and is a good source of fiber, vitamin C, vitamin K, vitamin B6, and chromium.

Brussels Sprouts

While growing Brussels sprouts offers a true taste sensation, doing so can be a bit challenging in the warmer areas of SoCal. The plant requires cool temperatures to form sprouts and needs a long growing season before the sprouts are ready for harvest. If you live along the coast, you will likely have an easier time growing Brussels sprouts.

Wherever you are growing, plant as soon as the weather has cooled in fall. If you are located inland, look for heat tolerant, early-bearing varieties such as 'Jade Cross Hybrid'.

As with cauliflower and broccoli, the edible part of Brussels sprouts, which resemble small cabbages, are swollen flower buds. Unlike other members of the *Brassica* family, the plant is tall, reaching 2 to 3 feet. Sprouts form all the way up the stalk in a striking whorling pattern.

Nutritional Nugget:
Brussels sprouts pack a vitamin K and vitamin C punch at 150% and 250% of the daily target per cup, respectively. The fiber in Brussels sprouts supports digestive health and helps feed the beneficial gut bacteria, along with helping to regulate blood sugar.

Growing Tips

Growing Season:
Fall - Early Spring

Container Growing Candidate:
Yes. Minimum 15-gallon container for one plant.

Location:
Full sun (minimum 8 hours). Well-worked ground soil, container or raised bed.

Soil:
Rich, well-draining soil. Mix into the top 6 to 8 inches of clay soil a 2- to 3-inch layer of compost, if planting in the ground. Keep the growing area weed free.

Planting:
Plant transplants 15 to 24 inches apart once heat has passed. If you want to seed your own, do so in containers at the end of summer, allowing 4 to 5 weeks before planting in the garden.

Fertilizing:
Fertilize at planting time with an organic, well-balanced, dry vegetable fertilizer. In early spring, apply an organic, well-balanced, liquid fertilizer.

Watering:
Keep soil moist but not soggy. Avoid letting the soil dry out, as this can cause the plant to stop producing sprouts. Mulch to preserve soil moisture and keep the roots cool.

Abnormal Growth:
Loose tufts of leaves inside the sprouts.
Cause: Sprouts developed during weather that was too hot.

Diseases:
Downy Mildew, Bacterial Soft Rot.
Prevention: Plant disease-resistant varieties. Provide good air circulation. Plant in well-draining soil. Rotate crops.

Harvesting:
80 to 100 days after transplanting. If growing from seed, add an additional 4 to 5 weeks. Sprouts are ready for harvesting when the large leaves on the plant just begin yellowing. The sprouts should be smaller than a golf ball and firm. Snap off or cut sprouts from the bottom, moving up as they mature. Each plant will yield 50 to 100 Brussels sprouts. You'll be able to harvest for a month or longer.

Secret Growing Tip:
Choose a planting site sheltered from high winds, as Brussels Sprouts plants are top-heavy and will easily topple over. To ensure this doesn't occur, stake the plant.

Cooking Tip:
Cut leaves off stalk and rinse. Wrap in cling wrap and microwave 4-5 mins. Brush olive oil and/or maple syrup over sprouts/stalk. Roast stalk on its side in 350°F oven for 45 mins.

Cabbage

It's not much of a stretch to say that you haven't truly tasted a head of cabbage until you've grown your own. Crisp, crunchy and delicious, cabbage is sure to be one of the highlights of your cool-season garden.

Cabbage varieties are quite varied. In addition to the standard light-green types, the vegetable comes in many shades of green, as well as cream and purple hues. You'll find round, tightly layered heads, as well as cabbage that is pointy or open and flat. Leaf textures also run the gamut — from smooth to the crinkly, puckered leaves of the mildly-flavored savoy cabbage.

Like other members of the *Brassica* family, when the weather becomes warm, cabbage may bolt, sending up flower stalks. For this reason, it's important to pay careful attention to the cabbage variety you grow in regard to your location. If you're growing inland, opt for early varieties of cabbage that are ready for harvest in 60 to 75 days. If you're located along the coast, you can easily grow late season cabbage that develops large heads. These can take 120 days or more to mature.

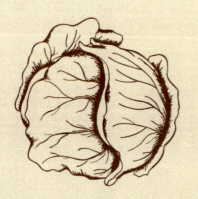

Nutritional Nugget:
Cabbage is filled with phytonutrients, especially red cabbage, which contains three carotenoids: lutein, zeaxanthin, and beta carotene. Carotenoids are pigments that give cabbage it's reddish-purple color, convert into vitamin A in the body, and give cabbage its antioxidant and anti-inflammatory properties. For added benefits, ferment homegrown cabbage to make sauerkraut or kimchi, which creates probiotics to nourish the bacteria in your gut and help digestion.

Growing Tips

Growing Season:
Fall - Winter
(Year-Round along Coast)

Container Growing Candidate:
No.

Location:
Full sun (minimum 8 hours). Well-worked ground soil or raised bed.

Soil:
Rich, well-draining soil. Mix into the top 6 to 8 inches of clay soil a 2- to 3-inch layer of compost, if planting in the ground. Keep the growing area weed free.

Planting:
Plant 15 to 24 inches apart. For best results, plant transplants from the nursery, or grow from seed and transplant in the garden when the cabbage is 3 inches tall. Plants started from seed indoors in mid-August will be ready for transplanting by early October. Plant late season varieties after heat has passed in fall and until mid-February for early season varieties. Cabbage can tolerate light frost. If heavy frost is predicted, cover the plant with floating row cover for the night.

Fertilizing:
Fertilize at planting time with an organic, well-balanced, dry vegetable fertilizer. A month after planting, begin fertilizing every 3 to 4 weeks with an organic, well-balanced, liquid fertilizer.

Watering:
Keep cabbage soil consistently moist but not soggy. Fluctuations in soil moisture levels can cause heads to split. Mulch to preserve soil moisture and keep the roots cool.

Diseases:
Root Rot, Club Root. (Latter more common in acidic soils).
Prevention: Avoid overwatering. Plant in well-draining soil. Rotate crops.

Secret Growing Tip:
In addition to standard cabbage, there is flowering cabbage. This highly ornamental variety of cabbage comes in striking color combinations, including cream, white, purple, and pink. Flowering cabbage is grown in the same manner as regular cabbage. What many people don't know, however, is that flowering cabbage leaves are edible, raw or cooked. They make a tasty, lovely addition to salads and stir-fries.

Harvesting:
60 to 120 days after transplanting. If the cabbage head bolts and flowers due to unseasonably warm weather, harvest the head as soon as possible before the flavor becomes compromised. Cut the cabbage head off at ground level with a sharp knife.

Carrots

Grow your own carrots, and you may never want to eat store-bought again. The crispy, sweet tang of these root crops is something you're not likely to forget. Pulling carrots out of the ground is also a delightful surprise for young gardeners. Clean the carrot well, and you and your little tyke can eat the carrot with the tops on.

The secrets to growing carrots in Southern California are to plant in the right kind of soil, stay ahead of Santa Ana winds and hot weather, water correctly, and have patience.

Southern California's clay soil is not amenable to carrots. Our soil is much too hard and compacted to allow these root vegetables to grow well. For that reason, it's best to simply plant carrots in containers or raised beds. In such growing situations, you can give carrots what they need, which is rich, well-draining soil that allows the root vegetable to easily grow and form.

When carrot plants are young, the soil surface drying out can kill the entire crop. That means you may need to water more than once a day during warm or windy weather.

Patience is a necessity when growing carrots, as they can take months to grow to full-size. Unlike some crops, there isn't a shortcut to growing them. They must be planted from seed. If you try to plant transplants, you'll find that they don't grow well, but instead become twisted and forked.

Varieties of carrots run the gamut, from small, bite-sized baby carrots—some shaped like golf balls—to standard Nantes types. While there are plenty of orange carrots, you'll also find yellow, red, and purple.

Nutritional Nugget:

The bright orange color of carrots comes from beta-carotene, an antioxidant your body converts into vitamin A—and the reason carrots are good for your eyesight!

Growing Tips

Growing Season:
Year-Round

Location:
Full sun (minimum 6 hours). Container or raised bed is best.

Container Growing Candidate:
Yes. Minimum 5-gallon container. Choose baby carrots for smaller containers. Any size carrot does well in large containers and beds.

Soil:
Rich, well-draining soil that is easily worked. SoCal clay soil does not work well for carrots. Compacted soil leads to little to no growth. If the carrots do grow, they will be forked, stunted, and hairy. If you live in an area with sandy soil, such as along the coast, bulk up the soil with compost so it is moisture retentive. If you wish to try growing in clay soil, add a 4- to 5-inch layer of compost and pumice to loosen up the soil.

Planting:
Sprinkle seeds onto the soil surface as evenly as possible. Then cover the seeds with a 1/8-inch layer of lightweight potting soil, seed starting mix or vermiculite. Water well with a fine mist of water. Cover the area with newspaper or burlap and soak the covering. The seeds take 2 to 3 weeks to germinate. During that time, keep the covering and soil surface moist. Once the tiny seedlings emerge, take off covering. When seedlings are 1-inch tall, thin to about 3 inches apart.

Fertilizing:
Fertilize at planting time with an organic, well-balanced, dry vegetable fertilizer. When plants reach 1- to 2-inches tall, water with an organic, well-balanced, liquid fertilizer every 4 weeks.

Watering:
Water young carrot plants when the soil surface is approaching dryness. If you wait until the soil surface is dry to touch, you may lose young plants, which have tiny root systems. Once carrot tops reach 3 inches tall, begin watering when the soil surface has dried. Your biggest enemy is water fluctuations. Try to maintain even watering. Too little water will lead to plant loss, while excessive watering discourages good color formation in the carrots and can lead to foliar disease. Additionally, wet-dry cycles will cause carrots to split.

Diseases:
Leaf Blight, Powdery Mildew.
Prevention: Avoid overhead watering later in the day. Ensure good air circulation. Keep the planting area weed free. Weeds can steal water from carrot plants and transmit diseases.

Secret Growing Tip:
An easy, safe way to thin carrots is to use garden shears to cut off the tops of unwanted plants. That way you don't disturb the roots of surrounding desired plants.

Harvesting:
60 to 120 days after seeding. How long it takes to get edible carrots will depend on the variety planted and the season in which you plant. Planting in late winter or early spring will lead to faster growth than if you plant in fall. To harvest, pull up on the carrot top, moving slightly back and forth as you do so. To check if the carrot is ready for harvest, stick your fingers in around the base of the carrot and feel. Carrots can be harvested at any size. The smaller the carrot, the more tender it will be.

Cauliflower

Tasty, homegrown cauliflower is something worth treasuring. For one, it's not easy to grow a big head of cauliflower in SoCal gardens.

Of all the *Brassica* veggies, this one is the most susceptible to temperature fluctuations. Cauliflower grows best when the weather is cool and a bit on the humid side. While this is certainly possible during our winter months, one hot day or Santa Ana wind spell will raise the temperature exponentially, and quickly suck humidity out of the air. When temperatures rise, cauliflower heads mature prematurely and stop growing, leaving you with a small head.

In addition to white types of cauliflower, you'll find green and purple varieties. To keep the white-headed varieties white, you need to blanch the plants. This refers to wrapping the cauliflower leaves around the head as it develops. Keeping the sun off the head will ensure it remains white. Self-blanching varieties also exist. With these types, the leaves automatically wrap themselves around the head.

Mini Cauliflower Sautéed in Butter & Garlic

Nutritional Nugget:

Thanks to paleo and low-carb diets, cauliflower has become a staple grain replacement, e.g. riced cauliflower. But cauliflower is more than a low-calorie, fiber-rich option with a mild flavor. It's also packed with nutrients! One cup of cauliflower has almost a full day's needs of vitamin C and is a good source of choline and vitamin K.

Growing Tips

Growing Season:
Fall - Winter

Container Growing Candidate:
Yes. Minimum 10-gallon container.

Location:
Full sun (minimum 6 hours). Well-worked ground soil, container or raised bed.

Soil:
Rich, well-draining soil. Mix into the top 6 to 8 inches of clay soil a 2- to 3-inch layer of compost, if planting in the ground. Keep the growing area weed free.

Planting:
Plant 15 to 24 inches apart. For best results, plant transplants from the nursery, or grow from seed and transplant in the garden when the plants are 3 inches tall. Plant after heat has passed in fall through early winter. Cauliflower plant stems tend to be crooked toward the base of the plant and fragile. Remove the bottom sets of leaves and plant to cover the crook. This will ensure that the plant stands up straight and grows strong.

Fertilizing:
Fertilize at planting time with an organic, well-balanced, dry vegetable fertilizer. A month after planting, begin fertilizing every 3 to 4 weeks with an organic, well-balanced, liquid fertilizer.

Watering:
Keep cauliflower soil moist but not soggy. Avoid letting the soil dry out, as this can cause the head to prematurely stop forming. Mulch to preserve soil moisture and keep the roots cool.

Diseases:
Downy Mildew, Club Root. (Latter more common in acidic soils).
Prevention: Increase air circulation. Plant disease-resistant varieties. Rotate crops.

Secret Growing Tip:
To quickly and easily blanch a cauliflower head, gather the leaves and secure them with a clothespin. This will keep sunlight from getting to the head. Blanch heads as soon as they begin developing.

Harvesting:
55 to 100 days after planting and 1 to 3 weeks after blanching. If your cauliflower head stops developing early due to weather conditions, harvest as soon as possible and enjoy. Even small heads can be tasty. Cut through the stalk with a sharp knife to harvest.

Riced Cauliflower

Celery

Crisp celery is a delicious treat fresh out of the garden, and much juicier than you've ever experienced. Grow your own, and you'll enjoy sweet, tangy stalks, rather than the stringy, sometimes bitter vegetable you'll find in the market.

Celery requires a long, cool growing season, so plant as soon as the weather cools in fall. That way the plant has time to reach maturity before spring.

Raising celery from seed is a long process, so for best results, use transplants. Older varieties of celery require blanching to keep the stalks white. Newer types are self-blanching.

Nutritional Nugget:

Widely recognized as one of the healthiest snacks available, celery is hydrating, rich in fiber, and a great source of nutrients, including vitamins A, K, and C, plus minerals like potassium and folate. Low on the glycemic index, celery has a slow effect on blood sugar and is packed with antioxidants.

Celeriac:

Often called celery root, celeriac is grown for its round, edible root that tastes like mild celery. You peel the root and use cooked in soups and stews, and raw in salads and slaws. Grow celeriac the same as celery, except they must be planted from seed. Transplanting leads to poorly shaped roots. Harvest when the root is 3 to 5 inches in diameter, which will generally be 100 to 120 days after planting.

Growing Tips

Growing Season:
Late Fall - Winter

Container Growing Candidate:
No.

Location:
Full sun (minimum 6 hours). Well-worked ground soil or a raised bed.

Soil:
Rich, well-draining soil. Mix into the top 6 inches of soil a 2- to 3-inch layer of compost, if planting in the ground.

Planting:
Dig a trench 14 inches wide. Plant transplants 6 inches apart. Water deeply after planting.

Fertilizing:
Fertilize at planting time with an organic, well-balanced, dry vegetable fertilizer. Once the plants are six weeks old, begin applying an organic, liquid fertilizer every two weeks.

Watering:
Water frequently to keep the soil moist. Constant moisture will ensure the celery grows healthy and quickly. Plants will bolt and form seed heads if the soil dries out. Mulch to keep the soil moist.

Diseases:
Aster Yellows. **Prevention/Solution:** Remove infected plants. Control weeds. Treat for leafhoppers, which carry the disease.
Fungal Leaf Spot, Crown Rot. **Prevention/Solution:** Rotate crops. Remove plant debris promptly. Apply fungicide.

Secret Growing Tip:
Self-blanching celery varieties naturally develop white stalks, but older varieties require blanching. If you aren't sure what type of celery you're growing, it won't hurt to blanch the plant. To do so, a month before harvest, wrap the celery stalks in newspaper and secure with a rubber band. Mound earth around the base of the plant and continue watering and fertilizing.

Harvesting:
90 to 130 days after planting. Cut off outer individual celery stalks one-by-one at the soil line, or wait until all stalks have matured and dig up the plant.

72

Corn

Though corn requires considerable space to grow, making room is well worth the effort. Standard sweet corn's sugar turns to starch very quickly, so growing corn at home is the only way to experience just how sweet and tender corn can be.

Once you harvest corn from the garden, you'll want to immediately shuck it and steam or boil to lock in the sweet. Hybridizers have developed varieties that hold their sugar content longer, but they still pale in comparison to the homegrown tasting experience.

Kids find growing corn to be magical. Especially if you grow popcorn. This type of corn produces poppable kernels in a wide variety of fun colors, including red, yellow, black, pink, and white.

Popcorn:

Popcorn varieties require the same growing conditions and care as sweet corn. The main difference is that you must leave the popcorn ear on the plant until the entire stalk turns brown and kernels are hard and glossy. The kernels will only pop well if they are completely dry. Hang ears in a cool, dry place for at least 4 to 5 weeks after harvesting. Once the whole ear has dried, you can remove the kernels and store them in airtight jars for several months, or keep the dried cobs intact and place in a mesh bag after removing husks. To quickly and easily pop corn, stick the dried kernels or a corn cob in a clean paper bag and pop in the microwave on the popcorn setting or until there is 1 second between pops.

Growing Tips

Growing Season:
Spring - Summer

Container Growing Candidate:
No.

Location:
Full sun. In the ground or raised bed. Allow room to grow block plantings of corn in three to four short rows. Pollen from male flowers has to reach female silks. Wind will cross-pollinate the plants, which is needed for full ears of corn to develop.

Soil:
Rich, well-draining, loose soil. Mix into the top 8 to 10 inches of soil a 4- to 5-inch layer of compost. If the soil is particularly compacted, add a cup of pumice to improve drainage.

Planting:
Plant when weather warms in April through mid-June. If you plant later in summer, the corn ears may not have enough time to fully develop before the weather cools and days shorten. Position corn so it is north of other sun crops. Otherwise, when the corn plants grow tall, they'll cast shade on the rest of the garden. Sow corn seeds directly in the ground, or plant transplants. Plant seeds in the ground starting in April, or in containers indoors in March to transplant when the weather warms. Plant 1 foot apart in rows that are 3 feet apart.

Fertilizing:
Fertilize at planting time with an organic, well-balanced, dry vegetable fertilizer. Feed again with an organic, high-nitrogen liquid fertilizer when the stalks reach 12 to 15 inches tall. Repeat when the stalks are 2 to 2 1/2 feet tall.

Watering:
When seeding in the ground, water the planting area well initially and then only water when the soil surface has dried. Soggy seeds may rot rather than sprout. Once the corn plant is growing, however, keep the planting area consistently moist. If the soil is too dry, the plant won't produce or ears won't form well. When the plant reaches 4 inches tall, mulch to conserve soil moisture.

Diseases:
Maize Dwarf Mosaic Virus.

Prevention/Solution: Plant disease-resistant varieties. Control weeds and aphids. Destroy and discard affected plants. Clean hands and tools after touching infected plants before handling healthy ones.

Rust. **Prevention/Solution:** Plant disease-resistant varieties. Treat with fungicide. Avoid overhead watering late in day.

Secret Growing Tip:
Grow supersweet varieties at least 400 yards away from standard sugary and sugar enhanced varieties. Cross-pollination of these two types of corn results in supersweet ears with starchy, tough kernels.

Harvesting:
60 to 100 days after planting. Sweet corn is usually ready for harvest 17 to 24 days after the first silk strands appear. Harvest when husks are still green, silks have dried out and browned, and the kernels are full-sized and plump all the way to the tip of the ear. To ensure the ear is ready, puncture a kernel. Milky liquid should come out. If the liquid is clear, the corn isn't ready for harvesting. If no liquid emerges, it's too late.

Nutritional Nugget:
While corn can sometimes be seen as a less healthy vegetable because of its use in chips and other fried foods due to its high starch content, corn is also a whole grain rich in fiber and other plant compounds that can aid in digestion and eye health. Corn provides our bodies with essential vitamins and minerals such as B vitamins, vitamin C, magnesium, and copper. Corn seed grown in home gardens is not genetically modified.

Cucumbers

In addition to offering a wide variety of taste sensations, cucumbers come in many shapes, sizes, and colors. You'll find cukes for slicing and cukes for pickling, the latter of which have been bred to fit in jars. Enjoy short, warty cucumbers and long, ribbed or smooth ones. Tastes also vary, from mild, to bold, to lemony. Some older varieties of cucumber cause burps, but there are now burpless types.

While all vegetables require pollination, cucumbers and other members of the cucurbit family, including squash and pumpkin, often experience pollination problems. This occurs because plants in this family grow male and female flowers that require cross-pollination for fruit development.

Be advised that the first flowers on the cucumber plant are male, and these often quickly fall off. Don't be alarmed, though. Female flowers will soon bloom, as well as more male flowers. At this point, it's important that bees cross-pollinate the flowers. If it looks like you might not have enough bees pollinating your cucumbers, you can pollinate yourself. Stick a small paintbrush inside a male flower and twirl it around; then insert the paintbrush into a female flower. Female flowers contain immature fruit, and male flowers are shorter.

Cucamelons:

Though not in the cucurbit family, cucamelons have a cucumber taste with overtones of lemon. Resembling little watermelons, these cute little fruit are easy to grow and prolific, providing plenty of fruit over the growing season. They require the same growing conditions as regular cucumbers, including trellising.

Growing Tips

Growing Season:
Spring - Summer

Container Growing Candidate:
Yes. Minimum 15-gallon container.

Location:
Full sun. In the ground, raised bed or container.

Soil:
Rich, well-draining soil. Mix into the top 4 to 8 inches of soil a 2- to 3-inch layer of compost. If the soil is particularly compacted, add pumice to improve drainage.

Planting:
Plant when the weather warms in early April through July. Sow seeds directly into the ground or in containers and plant transplants when they reach 2 to 3 inches tall. Seeds can be started indoors in March for transplanting in April. Bush cucumber plants can grow without support, but vining varieties require a trellis, cage or fence to grow on. Plant 1 to 3 feet apart.

Fertilizing:
Fertilize at planting time with an organic, well-balanced, dry vegetable fertilizer. Once the plant begins growing, feed every 3 to 4 weeks with an organic fertilizer high in potassium, such as a 0-0-22. Langbeinite is a good organic source of potassium.

Watering:
Given the fact that cucumbers consist of mostly water, the plants require consistent moisture, especially when fruit has formed. If watering is inconsistent, the fruit may become bitter. Soak the planting area well when the top of the soil dries out. Also keep the area weed free, as weeds steal water.

Diseases:
Angular Leaf Spot. **Prevention:** Avoid wetting foliage when watering.
Powdery Mildew. **Prevention/Solution**: Destroy infected plants. Dust with sulfur. Plant disease-resistant varieties.

Secret Growing Tip:
If your cucumber plant fails to flower, you may be overfertilizing. High doses of nitrogen will cause cucumbers to produce healthy foliage but no fruit. Refrain from fertilizing, and the plant is likely to begin flowering.

Harvesting:
50 to 70 days after planting. Pick cucumbers when they are 2 to 10 inches long, depending on the variety. Harvest before the cucumber turns yellow, as the taste is compromised at that point. Harvesting regularly keeps cucumber plants producing longer.

Nutritional Nugget:
Cucumbers are mostly water but packed with electrolytes, making the vegetable a hydrating and refreshing snack that can prevent dehydration. They are low in calories and a good source of vitamin C, vitamin K, magnesium, potassium, and manganese. Place cut slices on your skin to reduce swelling and irritation or to alleviate sunburns.

Eggplant

Eggplant makes a lovely addition to the summer vegetable garden. The plant grows 2 to 3 feet tall and features purple or white, star-shaped flowers with striking yellow stamens. The blooms develop into black, purple, green or white glossy fruit. You'll find standard-sized, 8-inch-long eggplant and shorter, more slender varieties. Some of the smaller eggplants are the size and shape of eggs.

Eggplant thrives during SoCal's warm weather. Plant this heat-lover in spring when the weather warms, and you can enjoy harvesting eggplant until fall. Use the bounty of your harvest to create a variety of tasty dishes, including culinary classics like Moussaka and Eggplant Parmesan.

Nutritional Nugget:
Eggplant is a nutrient-dense food, meaning the vegetable has a good amount of fiber, vitamins, and minerals, while being low in calories. Eggplant contains manganese, copper, vitamin B6, and thiamine, along with anthocyanins, a purple pigment with antioxidant function.

Mandy's Turkey & Eggplant Mozzarella

Ingredients:
1 large eggplant, cut into 1/4" slices
1 28-oz can tomatoes
1 teaspoon olive oil
1 medium onion, finely chopped
3 cloves garlic, minced
8-oz ground turkey
1 8-oz can tomato sauce
1 1/2 teaspoons dried oregano
1/4 teaspoon cayenne
1 cup shredded mozzarella
1/2 cup breadcrumbs
2 tablespoons parmesan cheese

Instructions:
Coat a baking sheet with olive oil. Lay eggplant slices on sheet and bake at 350°F for 20 to 25 mins, until softened. Let cool. While eggplant is cooking, puree tomatoes with liquid in a food processor or blender. Heat olive oil in a large skillet over medium. Add onion and garlic; sauté 15 mins. Add ground turkey, breaking up. Cook through. Add pureed tomatoes, tomato sauce, and spices. Simmer for 25 mins.
In a 9"x13" pan, spoon a little of the sauce mixture. Then place half the eggplant slices over this and spoon half the sauce mixture over eggplant, followed by all of the mozzarella cheese. Layer remaining eggplant and sauce. Combine breadcrumbs and parmesan, then sprinkle on top. Bake at 350°F for 30 mins. Let sit 10 mins before eating.
Makes 6 servings.

Growing Tips

Growing Season:
Spring - Summer

Container Growing Candidate:
Yes. Minimum 15-gallon container.

Location:
Full sun. In the ground, raised bed or container.

Soil:
Rich, well-draining soil. Mix into the top 4 to 8 inches of soil a 2- to 3-inch layer of compost. If the soil is particularly compacted, add pumice to improve drainage.

Planting:
Plant when the weather warms in early April through July. Though you can sow seeds directly into the ground, it's easier to seed plants in containers and plant transplants when they reach 2 to 3 inches tall. Seeds can be started indoors in March for transplanting in April. Plant 3 feet apart.

Fertilizing:
Fertilize at planting time with an organic, well-balanced, dry vegetable fertilizer. A month after planting, begin fertilizing every 4 weeks with an organic, well-balanced, liquid fertilizer.

Watering:
Water often to maintain moist but not soggy soil. Avoid letting the soil dry out. Mulch to keep the soil moist.

Diseases:
Mosaic Viruses. **Prevention:** Plant disease-resistant varieties.
Spotted Wilt Virus. **Prevention:** Spreads by thrips, which live in and also infect weeds, so control weeds.
Verticillium Wilt. **Prevention:** Plant disease-resistant varieties indicated by a V for Verticillium. Remove and dispose of infected plants following harvest. Avoid planting tomatoes, peppers, eggplant, and potatoes in the same area for four years. If growing space is limited or you're growing in raised beds, remove 1 to 2 feet of soil and replace with soil from another raised bed or area of the garden.

Secret Growing Tip:
If you still have eggplant ripening in fall when the weather is starting to cool, cover the plant with floating row cover at night to hasten ripening.

Harvesting:
60 to 90 days after planting. Use a knife or pruning shears to harvest eggplant when it is glossy and filled out and the flesh no longer springs back when pressed. Make sure to harvest before eggplant loses its shine and becomes dull. At that point, the vegetable will taste bitter and have a dry, leathery texture. The more often you pick eggplant, the more it will grow.

Garlic

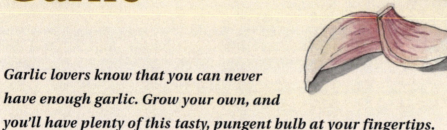

Garlic lovers know that you can never have enough garlic. Grow your own, and you'll have plenty of this tasty, pungent bulb at your fingertips.

   There are two main types of garlic — hardneck and softneck. Hardneck garlic is intensely-flavored and less commonly found in the grocery store than softneck. Softneck types have smaller cloves than hardnecks and are easily braided after harvest.

   Patience is necessary when growing garlic, as it takes a full 9 to 10 months for bulbs to reach maturity. Bulbs don't even form underground until the leaves have grown above ground for 5 to 6 months.

Easy Roasted Garlic

Ingredients:
1 or more whole heads of garlic
Extra virgin olive oil

Instructions:
Preheat your oven (or toaster oven) to 400°F.
Peel and discard the papery outer layers of the whole garlic bulb, leaving the skins of each clove intact.
Cut 1/4" to 1/2" from the top of the garlic head to expose individual cloves.
Place garlic head(s) in baking pan or muffin tin, cut side up (or garlic roaster/baker if you have one).
Drizzle 1-2 tsp olive oil over the exposed top.
Cover each bulb with aluminum foil (not needed when using roaster with lid).
Bake at 400°F for 30-40 mins, or until the cloves are lightly browned and feel soft when pressed. You can continue roasting until deeply golden.
Let the garlic cool slightly, then press the bottom of each clove to push it out of its paper.
Serve immediately, or refrigerate for up to 2 weeks.

Nutritional Nugget:

Mainly known for its flavor in cooking, garlic has been used throughout history as a medicine. Its antifungal and antibacterial properties can be credited to the presence of the sulphur-containing compound, Allicin.

Freshly Picked Braided Garlic

Growing Tips

Growing Season:
Fall - Early Summer

Container Growing Candidate:
Yes. Minimum 10-gallon container.

Location:
Full sun (minimum 6 hours). Container or raised bed is best.

Soil:
Rich, well-draining soil. Add a 2- to 3-inch layer of compost if planting in the ground in clay soil. Ensure that the planting area is free of any impediments, such as stones and sticks. Keep the growing area weed free.

Planting:
Although you can plant supermarket garlic, you'll have better germination rates by planting bulbs from a nursery or garden center. Plant individual cloves 1 inch deep with the pointed tip up and just below the soil surface. Space 4 to 6 inches apart in the ground and 3 inches apart in containers and raised beds.

Fertilizing:
Fertilize at planting time with an organic, well-balanced, dry vegetable fertilizer. In spring, begin applying an organic, well-balanced, liquid fertilizer monthly.

Watering:
Water garlic deeply but infrequently. If the soil stays too moist, the bulbs may rot. Water when the top 2 inches of soil have dried out.

Diseases:
Pink Root, Downy Mildew. **Prevention:** Provide good air circulation. Rotate crops. Remove and destroy old plant vegetation. Avoid overwatering.

Secret Growing Tip:
Once garlic cloves have cured, which refers to the outer skins becoming dry and papery and there is no longer any green, you can use some of the cloves to plant your next batch.

Harvesting/Storage:
9 to 10 months after planting. You will know it's time for harvesting when the plant's leaf tips start to turn yellowish-brown. At that point, stop watering and press the foliage flat against the ground. This will prevent the tops from flowering, and the bulbs will mature more quickly. Harvest when the leaves are mostly brown. Lift out the bulbs with a garden fork. If you yank the plants out by hand, you can crack the bulbs, decreasing storage life. Cure (dry) bulbs outdoors in a basket or braid the foliage and hang to dry. Wait until the skins are papery. This will take 2 to 3 weeks, depending on the weather. Once they are dry, remove any dirt, cut off most of the roots, and store the bulbs in a mesh bag or braided. Hang in a cool, dry, well-ventilated location away from direct sun.

Greens for Stir-Fry

The mainstays of most stir-fries, greens add interest and good taste to the garden. Most stir-fry greens are quick-maturing, cool-season plants harvested when foliage is young and tender. Many stir-fry greens, such as Swiss chard, also make decorative additions to the garden. The chard cultivar 'Bright Lights', for instance, decorates the landscape with large green leaves featuring neon red, orange, pink, and yellow veining and stems.

Some greens like mizuna have serrated leaves, while others such as many mustard greens tend to be frilly. In the case of bok choy, also known as pak choi, the plant has a white, bulbous bottom that you cut up and stir-fry in addition to the leaves. Another green that has a similar growth pattern and use is napa cabbage.

Nutritional Nugget:
Dark, leafy greens are rich in phytonutrients, including antioxidants. Bok choy, for example, contains the flavonoid quercetin, which can help to reduce inflammation in the body. Stir-fry greens are great sources of vitamins A, C and K, along with minerals potassium, iron, and magnesium. Stir-frying retains more nutrients than boiling and results in tender-crisp vegetables without much added oil/fat. The process also makes the fat-soluble vitamins and several plant compounds more absorbable.

Growing Tips

Growing Season:
Fall - Spring
(Year-Round along Coast)

Container Growing Candidate:
Yes. Minimum 10-gallon container.

Location:
Full sun or partial shade.

Soil:
Rich, well-draining soil. If planting in the ground, loosen clay soil by mixing in a 3-inch layer of compost into the top 6 inches of soil. Bulk up sandy soil by mixing in a 4-inch layer of compost into the top 6 inches of soil. Keep growing area weed free.

Planting:
Seed directly in the garden or plant in containers and transplant when the seedlings are 2 to 4 inches tall. Sow seed 1/4 to 1/2 inch deep, depending on plant type. When sowing directly, space seed 3 inches apart, thinning to 6 to 12 inches apart, depending on the plant.

Fertilizing:
Fertilize at planting time with an organic, well-balanced, dry vegetable fertilizer. A month after planting, begin fertilizing monthly with an organic, well-balanced, liquid fertilizer.

Watering:
Water stir-fry greens when the soil surface has dried. Keep soil consistently moist during seed germination and until seedlings reach 1 to 2 inches tall.

Diseases:
Most stir-fry greens are members of the *Brassica* family of plants. These include mustard, bok choy, collards, mizuna, and napa cabbage. See kale and cabbage for disease susceptibility and prevention.

Secret Growing Tip:
While many greens are harvested young, it's a good practice to sample greens at various stages of growth to determine which tastes best. Peak flavor and tenderness varies among stir-fry greens.

Harvesting:
Harvest greens when young and tender. This is generally when the foliage is 2 to 4 inches in length. Pick older greens first.

Kale

One of the most decorative and delicious members of the Brassica family, kale produces rosettes of leaves in various colors and textures. You'll find kale leaves that are smooth, while others are bumpy, and some are curly. Color variations include shades of green and purple.

Kale is a cool-season plant. Cold days and nights, and even a touch of frost, give kale leaves a sweet flavor. While kale will continue to grow when the weather is warm, the leaves won't be as sweet. A hot spell during the growing season can cause kale leaves to turn bitter. Once it cools down again, kale will resume growing sweet leaves.

Kale is among one of the easiest plants to grow in the *Brassica* family. Keep the plant healthy, and you can continue to harvest tasty leaves for months.

Nutritional Nugget:
Kale is known as the leafy green full of vitamins and is one of the most nutrient-dense foods on the planet! One of the best sources of Vitamin K, kale is chock-full of antioxidants and minerals, too. While not as rich a source of Alpha-Linoleic Acid (ALA) as fish, kale boasts 121mg ALA per cup; this Omega-3 fatty acid is essential for brain health.

Collards:

Collards are a type of kale that has smooth, gray-green leaves resembling cabbage. The plant grows best in the cool season, but like kale can be grown during the warmer months of the year. Grow collards in the same manner as kale.

Growing Tips

Growing Season:
Fall - Early Summer

Container Growing Candidate:
Yes. Minimum 5-gallon container for one plant.

Location:
Full sun to light shade. In the ground, raised bed or container.

Soil:
Rich, well-draining soil. Mix into the top 6 inches of clay soil a 2- to 3-inch layer of compost, if planting in the ground. Keep the area weed free.

Planting:
Plant 12 to 24 inches apart. You can direct seed kale in the garden, but they will take twice as long to germinate than starting them in containers and then transplanting. Kale transplants can generally be found in the nursery fall through spring.

Fertilizing:
Fertilize at planting time with an organic, well-balanced, dry vegetable fertilizer. When plants reach 3 to 4 inches tall, water with an organic, well-balanced, liquid fertilizer every 3 to 4 weeks.

Watering:
Keep the soil around young kale plants moist but not soggy. Water mature kale plants when the top inch of soil has dried out. Do a deep soak when watering.

Diseases:
Damping-Off, Fusarium Wilt. **Prevention:** Plant disease-resistant varieties. Provide good air circulation. Plant in well-draining soil. Rotate crops.

Secret Growing Tip:
The leaves of kale are so ornamental that you can grow the vegetable as a decorative edible.

Harvesting:
45 to 75 days after planting. Pick off outer leaves as soon as they grow large enough to eat.

Cooking Tip:
When you have a lot of kale, it's a great addition to stir-fries or pasta dishes!
Strip kale leaves from ribs and stems, then tear leaves crosswise into 2"-3" pieces.
Heat a few tablespoons of olive oil in a skillet over medium heat. Add kale in batches and toss. Cover and sauté for 5 mins, stirring occasionally. Season with salt, pepper, and red chili flakes, sautéing 2-3 more mins. Serve or add to dish.

Kohlrabi

Resembling a small spacecraft on "Star Trek" hovering over the garden soil, kohlrabi is a lesser-known cool-season vegetable definitely worth growing. While the leaves and leafstalks of this member of the Brassica family are edible, it's the swollen, bulbous stem that is most often enjoyed. Kohlrabi features a mild flavor and crisp texture compared to other plants in the same family, such as turnips.

Kohlrabi comes in a striking purple color, as well as white and green. Use this delicious vegetable for a wide variety of culinary uses. For instance, Kohlrabi adds a crunchy, pleasant taste to salads and slaws. You can also cook, sauté and steam the vegetable and add it to stir-fries and soups. The leaves and stems taste like tangy cabbage. Of all *Brassica* plants, kohlrabi is by far one of the easiest to grow. These fast-growing plants are ready to harvest in just 50 to 60 days.

Nutritional Nugget:
Like other cruciferous vegetables, kohlrabi is a good source of dietary fiber, which improves digestive health. Providing manganese, copper, potassium, vitamin B6, and lots of vitamin C, this veggie may be lesser known, but it's sure full of nutrients!

Kohlrabi Slaw

2 kohlrabi (medium-size), peeled and shredded
2 tablespoons fresh lemon juice
2 cloves garlic, crushed
3 tablespoons mayonnaise
Salt and pepper to taste

Combine all ingredients and refrigerate for 3 hours. Makes 4 to 6 servings.

Growing Tips

Growing Season:
Fall - Spring

Container Growing Candidate:
Yes. Minimum 10-gallon container for one plant.

Location:
Full sun. In the ground, raised bed or container.

Soil:
Rich, well-draining soil. Mix into the top 6 inches of clay soil a 2- to 3-inch layer of compost, if planting in the ground. Keep the area weed free.

Planting:
Plant seed indoors in August for transplanting into the garden in September or sow seed directly in the garden in fall when the weather has cooled. When seedlings reach 2 to 3 inches tall, thin to 4 to 6 inches apart. Overcrowding will cause the bulbs to not develop well. Because kohlrabi is fast-growing, you can enjoy several crops throughout the growing season by seeding every 2 weeks for the first 2 months.

Fertilizing:
Fertilize at planting time with an organic, well-balanced, dry vegetable fertilizer. When plants reach 3 to 4 inches tall, water with an organic, well-balanced, liquid fertilizer once. Too much nitrogen can cause the stems to grow at the expense of the bulbs.

Watering:
Keep kohlrabi soil consistently moist but not soggy. A lack of water early on can lead to the plant not forming a bulb. Mulch to preserve soil moisture and keep the roots cool.

Diseases:
Root Rot, Club Root. (Latter more common in acidic soils). **Prevention:** Avoid overwatering. Plant in well-draining soil. Rotate crops.

Secret Growing Tip:
If kohlrabi splits, that is an indication of too much nitrogen fertilizer or underwatering.

Harvesting:
50 to 60 days after planting. Harvest when kohlrabi is 2 to 3 inches in diameter. If you wait until kohlrabi grows any larger, it may taste overly spicy and be fibrous. Peel, slice, and serve raw or cooked. Young leaves and leafstalks taste best when they're steamed before serving.

Leeks

Long favored by chefs for their mild, sweet onion flavor, leeks are a tasty addition to your vegetable garden. Rather than forming a distinct bulb like its onion relative, leeks grow a stem resembling a long green onion. The edible stalk, which grows 6 to 8 inches long and up to 2 inches thick, is not a true stem. It is actually a bundle of leaf sheaths.

Leeks grow best in SoCal's cool season. Growing them takes some patience. Leeks require 4 to 5 months to mature in the garden. To maintain the white color and mild flavor at the base of the leek, it's also necessary to blanch the plant to block out light. This is accomplished by mounding soil as the plant grows just under the bottom set of leaves.

Potato Leek Soup

Ingredients:
4 to 5 leeks, cleaned and sliced, dark green sections removed (use green portion for another use or discard)
2 teaspoons olive oil
4 medium white potatoes, washed and cut into cubes
1 32-oz carton chicken broth
1/2 cup water
3 bay leaves
1/2 tablespoon chicken bouillon
1/2 cup heavy cream or half-and-half
Salt and pepper to taste

Instructions:
Sauté leeks in olive oil until tender. Add potatoes, chicken broth, water, bay leaves, and bouillon. Simmer on medium until potatoes are tender. Turn off stove and wait until mixture cools enough to blend in a food processor (or blend directly in pot with immersion blender). Return to low heat and stir in cream or half-and-half. Bring just to a boil and turn off heat. Season to taste with salt and pepper.
Makes 4 to 6 servings.

Nutritional Nugget:

Leeks are rich in flavonoids (antioxidants), especially one called kaempferol, which have been shown to reduce the risk of chronic diseases. Low in calories and rich in flavor, leeks also contain vitamin K, manganese, and copper.

Growing Tips

Growing Season:
Fall - Spring

Container Growing Candidate:
Yes. Minimum 10-gallon container.

Location:
Full sun (minimum 6 hours).

Soil:
Rich, well-draining soil. Add a 3- to 4-inch layer of compost if planting in the ground in clay soil. If drainage is poor, add pumice. Keep the growing area weed free. Bulk up sandy soil with compost.

Planting:
Leeks are best grown by seeding in containers and transplanting in the garden when the plant reaches the diameter of a pencil. You may also be able to find leek transplants in the nursery or home and garden center. If you live inland, look for early season leek seed that is ready to harvest in 70 to 90 days, so that the plant matures before the weather becomes too warm in spring. Sow seeds in containers 6 to 8 weeks before transplanting. Plant in the garden starting in September when the weather has cooled. Plant 2 to 4 inches apart.

Fertilizing:
Fertilize at planting time with an organic, well-balanced, dry vegetable fertilizer. In spring, begin applying an organic, well-balanced, liquid fertilizer monthly.

Watering:
Keep leek soil consistently moist but not soggy. Leeks are shallow rooted, so you don't want the top 1 to 2 inches of soil to dry out at any point.

Diseases:
Downy Mildew, Purple Blotch. **Prevention:** Provide good air circulation. Rotate crops. Remove and destroy old plant vegetation. Plant disease-resistant varieties. Avoid watering and wetting foliage later in the day.

Secret Growing Tip:
When growing leeks in containers, fill the container 2/3 full of soil initially when planting. Once the leek begins to grow and the stem fattens up to the size of a pencil, begin blanching by mounding soil around the base of the plant just under the first set of leaves. Continue to mound soil as the plant grows. This will keep the bottom portion of the leak white, mild, and tender.

Harvesting/Storage:
4 to 5 months after planting. Harvest when stems are 1/2 to 2 inches thick. Remove leeks from the ground with a spading fork and shake off soil. Prepare for cooking by cutting off most of the roots. Then cut the leaves diagonally 6 to 8 inches above the stem. Separate layers when washing leeks.

Lettuce

On a cool fall or winter day, few harvests are as refreshing as crisp lettuce straight from the garden. You might pay a premium for organically grown greens in the store, but it's easy to grow your own tasty salad.

There are many types of lettuce from which to choose. You'll find lettuces in a variety of colors and shapes. Some have smooth, rounded leaves, while others are ruffled or serrated. The main types of lettuce to grow in the SoCal garden include butterhead, romaine, and cut-and-come-again loose leaf varieties. The latter category includes mesclun, a French-termed mix of various red and green loose leaf lettuces, chervil, endive, baby spinach, and various herbs.

Lettuce is a cool-season vegetable that thrives from late fall through spring in SoCal. Plant lettuce outdoors in late September, and you can enjoy refreshing greens into April. Lettuce grows well in containers, making it possible to cultivate your own salad bowl garden on a balcony, deck, or patio.

Nutritional Nugget:
One of the most widely consumed vegetables worldwide, lettuce's nutritional value is often underestimated. While a great base for low-calorie meals and full of water essential for hydration, lettuce also has a significant amount of vitamin A, along with smaller amounts of vitamin C, folate, and iron.

Growing Tips

Growing Season:
Fall - Spring
(Year-Round along Coast)

Container Growing Candidate:
Yes. Minimum 5-gallon container.

Location:
Part shade inland. Full sun along coast.

Soil:
Rich, well-draining soil. Add a 4- to 5-inch layer of compost if planting in the ground in clay soil. If drainage is poor, add pumice. Keep the growing area weed free. Bulk up sandy soil with compost.

Planting:
Plant lettuce seed indoors in August for transplanting into the garden in September or sow seed directly in the garden in fall when the weather has cooled. Lettuce seed is small. Sprinkle the seed on top of the soil and cover with a 1/4-inch layer of lightweight potting soil or seed starting mix. Keep the soil moist at all times during germination. When seedlings of heading lettuce types reach 2 to 3 inches tall, thin to 4 to 6 inches apart. With leaf lettuces, thinning is optional. For a succession of lettuce throughout the growing season, seed every 2 to 3 weeks until early spring.

Fertilizing:
Fertilize at planting time with an organic, well-balanced, dry vegetable fertilizer. A month after planting, begin applying an organic, well-balanced, liquid fertilizer every 2 to 3 weeks. Mix the fertilizer so it is 1/4 strength. You want nitrogen for leaf growth, but too much will lead to ammonia injury, causing root dieback and darkened leaves.

Watering:
Keep soil consistently moist but not soggy. Lettuce is a shallow rooted crop, so you don't want plants to dry out at any point. Once the leaves wilt, they often won't spring back. You also want to avoid overwatering, as too much moisture can lead to fungal diseases. Water when the soil surface has just dried out.

Diseases:
Downy Mildew, Sclerotinia Drop, Big Vein. **Prevention**: Provide good air circulation. Ensure excellent drainage. Rotate crops. Remove and destroy old plant vegetation. Plant disease-resistant varieties. Avoid watering and wetting foliage later in the day.

Secret Growing Tip:
Lettuce will bolt during hot, dry weather. This refers to the plant creating a flowerhead. When this occurs, the lettuce stops producing leaves, and the remaining leaves become bitter in taste. To prevent this from occurring during SoCal's inevitable "cool-season" hot spells, mulch around lettuce plants. On the days the weather becomes hot and dry, mist the plants several times a day.

Harvesting:
40 to 90 days after seeding, depending on variety. Loose leaf cut-and-come-again lettuce can be harvested as soon as the leaves are large enough to eat. Heading lettuces are ready when the heads are well-formed. Cut buttercrunch and romaine varieties off at the base of the plant. Snip off cut-and-come-again lettuce with scissors at ground level. They will grow back. Prevent wilting by picking lettuce during cool times of the day, such as morning and evening.

Onions

Growing your own onions, whether full-sized or scallions, gives you the opportunity to try many varieties. Enjoy white, yellow, and purple onions. Some mild and sweet types are perfect for eating raw, while others are bolder, adding complex flavors to cooked dishes.

To have success growing full-sized onions in SoCal, it's necessary to choose the proper variety. Onions are photothermoperiodic. That means they are sensitive to temperature, and even more importantly, day length. Onion plants are stimulated to stop producing foliage and begin forming bulbs in accordance with day length. Each variety only forms a bulb after it has received a certain amount of hours of sunlight each day for a specific number of days.

The number of hours of daylight required for full bulb growth varies greatly amongst onion varieties. They are therefore categorized into long-day, intermediate-day, and short-day varieties. The type of onion you want to plant in SoCal is short-day, also known as southern. The problem is the onion sets available at nurseries and home and garden centers are generally long-day. So, if you've tried to grow big onions from onion sets in SoCal and failed to get a good-sized onion, you were likely growing a long-day variety. The solution is to grow short-day varieties from seed, planting in early November. If you wish to grow green onions (scallions), plant onion sets fall through spring.

Green Onions:

If you wish to grow green onions (scallions) in SoCal, onion sets are the best method. These can be purchased in the nursery or home and garden center. They are small, immature onion bulbs usually of the long-day variety. They won't bulb up for you, but they will produce a bounty of tasty scallions. Harvest the whole green onion once the leaves are full and the bulb is 1/4 to 1/2 inch in diameter, or simply cut off leaves as needed, letting the plant continue to grow. The plant will produce ready-to-harvest leaves starting at just 2 weeks after planting.

Growing Tips

Growing Season:
Fall - Early Summer

Container Growing Candidate:
Yes. Minimum 10-gallon container.

Location:
Full sun.

Soil:
Rich, well-draining soil. Add a 3- to 4-inch layer of compost if planting in the ground in clay soil. If drainage is poor, add pumice. Keep the growing area weed free. Bulk up sandy soil with compost.

Planting:
Plant onions from sets (bulbs) or seed. To plant from sets, stick each individual onion set into the soil, tip side up, leaving the very top of the tip exposed. Space 1 to 2 inches apart. Water well after planting. To plant from seed, choose a short-day variety. Sow seed in containers for transplanting later or directly into the ground, raised bed or container. Plant seed 1/4 inch deep. Water well after seeding, and keep the soil moist during germination. When the seedlings are 1 inch tall, thin to 3 to 4 inches apart.

Fertilizing:
Fertilize at planting time with an organic, well-balanced, dry vegetable fertilizer. In spring, begin applying an organic, well-balanced, liquid fertilizer monthly.

Watering:
Keep onion soil consistently moist but not soggy. Onions are shallow rooted, so you don't want them to dry out at any point.

Diseases:
Pink Root, Downy Mildew, White Rot. **Prevention:** Provide good air circulation. Ensure excellent drainage. Rotate crops. Remove and destroy old plant vegetation. Plant disease-resistant varieties. Avoid watering and wetting foliage later in the day.

Secret Growing Tip:
Onions, including green onions, are biennials. That means if you plant green onions and choose to only use the tops the first year without harvesting the bulbs, you will have green onions growing continuously for two years. At the end of the second year, harvest the bulbs and enjoy them.

Harvesting:
3 to 5 months after planting for full-size onions. The foliage will begin yellowing and drying up when the onion is close to being ready for harvest. At that time, push the foliage flat against the ground. This forces the onion to reach the final stage of maturation. About 3 weeks later, the foliage should be fully withered. That indicates it's time to harvest. Use a spade or garden fork to dig up onions. They can be stored in the ground for a month or more, but remove immediately if you see new growth coming from the top. This indicates the plant is bolting, and that will cause the onion to shrivel up and become tough.

Nutritional Nugget:
Onions have been used for centuries as food and for their medicinal properties. These flavorful bulbs contain antioxidants and compounds that fight inflammation and promote beneficial gut bacteria, along with nutrients vitamin C, vitamin B6, and manganese.

Parsnips

The unique flavor of parsnips is even more pronounced when you grow this flavorful vegetable in your home garden. Sweet and creamy, this carrot relative tastes delicious when roasted or cooked and added to soups and stews.

For a successful harvest, parsnips require loose, well-draining soil free of impediments such as sticks and stones. Like carrots, parsnips will fork and split if the soil is too heavy. White or yellow in color, parsnips grow 12 to 15 inches long, depending on the variety. Because they take up to 4 months to grow into full-size, it's important to plant parsnips in the fall. You want this root vegetable to spend a good deal of time in the ground during winter. Cold nights and light frosts increase the sugar content in parsnips.

Parsnip Egg Casserole

Ingredients:
4 medium parsnips, shredded
1 pound sausage, cooked, crumbled and drained
2 cups cheddar cheese, shredded
1/4 cup onion, finely diced
1 bell pepper, diced (optional)
8 eggs
1 cup milk
1 teaspoon salt
1/2 teaspoon pepper

Instructions:
Preheat oven to 350°F and grease a 9×13 baking dish. Brown sausage, and drain fat. Layer shredded parsnips in baking dish, followed by browned sausage. Sprinkle cheese over top of sausage and parsnips. In a bowl, whisk eggs, onion, bell pepper, milk, salt, and pepper. Pour egg mixture into baking dish. Bake for 45-55 minutes or until eggs are set. Makes 8-10 servings.

Nutritional Nugget:
Parsnips contain both soluble and insoluble dietary fiber; soluble fiber being important for blood sugar control and insoluble fiber for digestive health and regularity. They are also a good source of vitamin C, vitamin E, folate, and copper!

Growing Tips

Growing Season:
Fall - Spring

Container Growing Candidate:
Yes. Minimum 15-gallon container. Choose shorter parsnip varieties.

Location:
Full sun. Container or raised bed is best.

Soil:
Rich, well-draining soil that is easily worked. Southern California clay soil does not work well for parsnips. Compacted, heavy soil leads to little to no parsnip growth. Parsnips that do grow will be forked and stunted. If you live in an area with sandy soil, such as along the coast, bulk up the soil with compost so that it is moisture retentive. If you wish to try growing in clay soil, add a 5- to 6-inch layer of homemade or bagged compost and pumice to loosen up the soil down to 18 inches.

Planting:
Sprinkle seeds onto the soil surface as evenly as possible. Then cover the seeds with a 1/4- to 1/2-inch layer of lightweight potting soil, seed starting mix or vermiculite. Water well with a fine mist of water and keep the area moist at all times. Parsnip seed takes 2 to 4 weeks to germinate, so patience is necessary. To help ensure that the planting area doesn't dry out during that time, cover the soil with newspaper or burlap and soak the covering. Keep the covering and soil moist. Once the tiny seedlings emerge, take off the covering. When seedlings are 1-inch tall, thin to 3 to 4 inches apart.

Fertilizing:
Fertilize at planting time with an organic, well-balanced, dry vegetable fertilizer. When plants reach 1- to 2-inches tall, water with an organic, well-balanced, liquid fertilizer every 4 weeks.

Watering:
Water young parsnip plants when the soil surface is approaching dryness. If you wait until the soil surface is dry to touch, you may lose young plants, which have tiny root systems. Once parsnip tops reach 4 inches tall, begin watering when the top 2 inches of soil have dried. Parsnips are much more drought-resistant than their carrot cousins.

Diseases:
None of note.

Secret Growing Tip:
Presoaking parsnip seeds in water for a day before planting can hasten germination. When it's time to plant, pour out the water and sprinkle seed on paper towels for 5 minutes to dry slightly. This will make it easier to handle the seeds for planting. Parsnip seeds don't store well, so plant a fresh batch each year.

Harvesting/Storage:
100 to 130 days after planting. When the foliage has died back, it's time to harvest. Dig parsnips out with a garden fork. Avoid leaving parsnips in the soil for an extended period once they're ready for harvest, as they can become tough and fibrous. You'll know this has occurred if the tops start going to seed.

Peanuts

Once known as double-jointed goober peas, peanuts grow underground, not on trees like other nuts. The plants produce bright-yellow flowers resembling sweet peas. When the flowers fade, stemlike shoots known as pegs develop at the base of the plant and burrow into the soil. These shoots then produce peanuts underground.

Peanuts thrive in SoCal's long, warm growing season. Plant peanuts in spring, and you'll have crops ready for harvesting in July or August. One peanut plant can produce as many as 50 to 60 peanut pods. There are four main types of peanuts. Virginia and runner types have two large seeds in each pod, whereas Spanish peanuts have two or three small seeds in each pod, and Valencia peanuts hold from three to six small nuts in each pod.

Nutritional Nugget:
Peanuts and peanut butter are one of the most nutrient-dense foods on the planet. This easy-to-prepare, affordable, shelf-stable product is widely used as a protein source around the world. Peanuts are an excellent source of healthful fats, protein, and fiber, along with containing potassium, iron, magnesium, phosphorus, and B vitamins.

Peanut Butter
Ingredients:
2 cups dry roasted peanuts
1-2 tablespoons honey or sugar (optional)
Sea salt to taste

Instructions:
Place peanuts in a food processor. Process until smooth, stopping to scrape sides every 1 minute. This will take 5-10 minutes total depending on how creamy you like it. Add honey/sugar and sea salt to taste. Store in the fridge or at room temperature if eaten within a couple of weeks. Makes about 1 cup of peanut butter.

Growing Tips

Growing Season:
Spring - Summer

Container Growing Candidate:
Yes. Minimum 15-gallon container for one plant.

Location:
Full sun. In the ground, raised bed or container.

Soil:
Rich, well-draining soil. It's important that the pegs are able to penetrate the surrounding soil and burrow in to grow peanuts. Sandy soil is ideal. Add compost to bulk up. If growing in clay soil, mix into the top 6 inches a 3- to 4-inch layer of compost. Peanut plants do especially well in containers and raised beds. Keep the area weed free.

Planting:
In spring, plant peanuts from peanut seeds (unroasted peanuts). Find them online or at the nursery. Plant each peanut seed with its skin intact 1 1/2 to 2 inches deep. Space Runner and Virginia peanuts 6 to 8 inches apart and Spanish and Valencia peanuts 4 to 6 inches apart.

Fertilizing:
Fertilize at planting time with an organic, well-balanced, dry vegetable fertilizer. When plants reach 5 to 6 inches tall, water with an organic, well-balanced, liquid fertilizer monthly.

Watering:
Keep soil consistently moist but not soggy. Stop watering two weeks before harvest when the plant's foliage has started to yellow.

Diseases:
Blight, Leaf Spot. **Prevention:** Provide good air circulation. Ensure excellent drainage. Rotate crops. Remove and destroy old plant vegetation. Avoid watering and wetting foliage later in day.

Secret Growing Tip:
Unroasted peanuts from the store will sometimes germinate and produce peanut plants.

Harvesting:
110 to 120 days after planting. Peanuts are ready to harvest when the plant's foliage has yellowed. Loosen the soil and dig up the plants, peanuts and all. Hang the entire plant in a warm, well-ventilated area in the shade and allow to dry for 2 to 3 weeks. When the foliage and peanuts have dried, strip the pods from the roots and discard the plants.

Peas

Pop a pea from the garden into your mouth and enjoy a burst of sweet goodness. The sugar in peas converts to starch just after harvesting, so growing your own is the only way to experience the true taste of this easy-to-grow legume.

As cool-season crops, peas thrive in SoCal gardens from late fall through early spring. They are quick to germinate from seed, which means you have time to grow more than one crop during the growing season. Pea plants are bush or vining types. Provide vining types with a trellis or wiring system to climb on, as they reach 6 to 8 feet tall or more. While bush types don't require support, they often do best with a small trellis that keeps the ripening pea pods off the ground.

Some peas you shell and eat, some have edible pods, and some can be enjoyed either way. Garden or shelling peas (also known as English peas) have a thin-skinned pod that you peel off to reveal plump peas. Sugar snap peas can be eaten unshelled, pod and all, or wait for the peas to develop more fully, and then shell them. Snow peas consist of a flat pod containing undeveloped pea seeds and are always eaten in their entirety.

55 days after planting:

85 days after planting:

Growing Tips

Growing Season:
Fall - Spring

Container Growing Candidate:
Yes. Minimum 15-gallon container.

Location:
Full sun.

Soil:
Rich, well-draining soil. Add a 3- to 4-inch layer of compost if planting in the ground in clay soil. If drainage is poor, add pumice. Keep the growing area weed free. Bulk up sandy soil with compost.

Planting:
Peas aren't usually high-yield plants, so for as bountiful a harvest as possible, plant a lot of plants, and try different varieties. For faster germination, soak pea seeds overnight the day before planting. Plant pea seeds indoors in August for transplanting into the garden in September when the plants reach 2 to 3 inches tall. Or wait and sow seed directly in the garden when the weather cools. Sow seed 1 inch deep. Ensure that the soil remains moist but not soggy during germination.

Fertilizing:
Pea plants need very little fertilizer. Feed plants just once about a month after planting with a well-balanced, liquid fertilizer.

Watering:
Keep soil around pea plants consistently moist but not soggy. Water when the soil surface dries.

Diseases:
Downy Mildew, Powdery Mildew, Fusarium Wilt.
Prevention: Provide good air circulation. Rotate crops. Remove and destroy old plant vegetation. Plant disease-resistant varieties. Avoid watering and wetting foliage later in the day.

Secret Growing Tip:
Peas are legumes and as such house nitrogen-fixing bacteria in their roots. That means growing peas enriches your garden soil for future crops. You can help peas fix even more nitrogen in the soil by applying a legume inoculant to the seeds at planting time.

Harvesting:
55 to 70 days after planting. Harvest shelling peas when pods have swelled and peas are just about round. Edible pod types should be harvested when the pods reach 2 to 3 inches long and before the seeds begin to swell. Eat peas soon after harvesting before the sugars turn to starch. Depending on weather, plants will produce peas for another 2 to 6 weeks.

Nutritional Nugget:
Sugar snap peas and snow peas are identical in their nutritional profiles and have less starches (carbohydrates) than your typical shelling peas. While the name makes them sound like they're full of sugar, the balance of fiber and protein with the naturally occurring sugars won't cause blood sugar level spikes. Their phytonutrient content, especially vitamin C, vitamin K, and folate, makes them a healthful snack!

Peppers

In addition to coming in a plethora of shapes, sizes and colors, peppers offer a wide range of taste sensations. Flavors range from mild and sweet to fruity, smoky, hot, and pungent. Pepper colors are bright and festive. You'll find peppers in yellow, orange, red, and many shades of green. With their shiny, deep green, pointy leaves and eye-catching fruit in a rainbow of colors, you can use pepper plants to decorate your spring and summer garden.

Peppers come in two main varieties. These are mildly flavored, large-fruited sweet bell types and hot chili peppers. Mild peppers include selections such as the standard bell, as well as banana, sweet cherry, and pimiento. In hot peppers you'll find many to choose from, including cayenne, serrano, habañero, jalapeño, Scotch bonnet, and Bhut Jolokia "Ghost Pepper". The large-fruited bell pepper types are mildly flavored, while hot peppers range from spicy to burn-up-your-mouth sizzling hot. Both types of peppers require the same care.

Peppers are considered hot-weather plants, but they produce the best during a fairly narrow temperature range. Fruit sets on sweet peppers best when nighttime temperatures are 60°F-75°F and daytime temperatures are 75°F. Chili peppers require a little hotter at 70°F-85°F. When it becomes hotter than 90°F, all peppers may drop blossoms without setting fruit.

Nutritional Nugget:

All varieties of peppers are excellent sources of vitamins A and C, potassium, folate, and fiber. The vitamin A supports vision health, and vitamin C supports immune health. Red peppers pack the most nutrition, as they stay longer on the vine before harvest. One cup of chopped red peppers contains nearly 3 times more vitamin C than an orange!

Growing Tips

Growing Season:
Spring - Summer

Container Growing Candidate:
Yes. Minimum 10-gallon container.

Location:
Full sun. In the ground, raised bed or container.

Soil:
Rich, well-draining soil. Mix into the top 4 to 8 inches of soil a 2- to 3-inch layer of compost. If the soil is particularly compacted, add pumice to improve drainage.

Planting:
Plant when the weather warms in early April through May. Though you can sow seeds directly into the ground, it's easier to seed plants in containers and plant transplants when they reach 2 to 3 inches tall. Seeds can be started indoors in February for transplanting in April. Plant 2 feet apart.

Fertilizing:
Fertilize at planting time with an organic, well-balanced, dry vegetable fertilizer. When blossoms set and open, fertilize with a half-strength solution of an organic, well-balanced, liquid fertilizer. If leaves are light green in color and you've been fertilizing, the plant may be deficient in magnesium. Spray the leaves with a solution of 1 teaspoon Epsom salt dissolved in a pint of warm water. Add a drop of surfactant to the mix, which will help the solution stick to the leaves.

Watering:
Water often to maintain moist but not soggy soil. Avoid letting the soil dry out — especially during flowering and fruiting.

Diseases:
Mosaic Virus, Spotted Wilt Virus, Verticillium Wilt. **Prevention**: Plant resistant varieties indicated by a V for Verticillium. Spotted Wilt Virus spreads by thrips, which live in and also infect weeds, so control weeds. Remove and dispose of infected plants following harvest. Rotate crops.

Harvesting:
60 to 95 days after planting. Pick when fruit are full size and well formed. The skin should be thick and crisp. If you wish to leave fruit on the plant to turn red, only leave one or two. Pepper plants with more than a few peppers on the plant will stop fruiting. Cut peppers at the stem with pruning shears or sharp scissors.

Secret Cooking Tip:
The heat in chili peppers is located in the seeds and the membrane inside the pepper. If you wish to cut down on the heat of the chili pepper before cooking, cut these portions out and discard them.

Potatoes

Potatoes add an exciting element to gardening. These tasty tubers grow underground, so digging them up at harvest time is like unearthing buried treasure. You'll find a wide range of potato varieties to plant in your garden. Enjoy red, brown, white, yellow, blue, and purple potatoes in flavors ranging from creamy and sweet to earthy. Shapes vary from fingerlike to round.

Like their tomato cousins, potato plants produce an abundance of sprawling vines aboveground. Unlike tomatoes, the crop forms underground as tubers, which are swollen underground stems.

Potatoes can be grown from seed potatoes that you cut up, or plant mini tubers. Whole mini tubers are less likely to rot — especially in clay soil. Growing potatoes involves "dirting" them, which requires that you mound up soil around the stems as they grow. The potatoes form off the buried stems.

Sweet Potatoes:

You may have grown sweet potato vines indoors. Did you know that SoCal's long warm season is ideal for growing these yummy tubers in your garden? Sweet potatoes require full sun and rich, well-draining soil that is easily worked. Get disease-free sweet potato slips (rooted cuttings) from a nursery or seed provider and plant in the spring. Sweet potato produces sprawling vines aboveground and potatoes underground. Water, fertilize and harvest as you would regular potatoes. Mounding soil on the stems is not necessary. Growing sweet potatoes is a nutritious undertaking. They are extremely high in vitamin A and an excellent source of potassium, manganese, vitamin B6, and fiber. Additionally, they are rich in antioxidants that protect your body, and, along with the fiber, contribute to good digestion and gut health. Unlike other starchy foods, sweet potatoes are relatively low on the glycemic index, which helps control blood sugar levels.

Growing Tips

Growing Season:
Fall - Spring

Container Growing Candidate:
Yes. Minimum 10-gallon container.

Location:
Full sun. Container or raised bed is best.

Soil:
Rich, well-draining soil that is easily worked. SoCal clay soil does not work well for potatoes. Compacted, heavy soil leads to little to no growth, deformed potatoes, or rotted tubers. If you live in an area with sandy soil, such as along the coast, bulk up soil with a 4- to 5-inch layer of compost to increase moisture retention. If you wish to try growing in clay soil, add a 5- to 6-inch layer of compost and pumice to loosen up soil.

Planting:
Plant September through April. Use seed potatoes or mini tubers. Cut seed potatoes into 1 1/2-inch chunks that have at least two eyes on them. For container growing, fill the the pot two-thirds full with high-quality potting soil. Place seed potatoes on the surface 4 to 5 inches apart. Cover with 2 to 3 inches of soil. For ground and raised bed growing, insert the seed potatoes into the soil 2 to 3 inches deep, spacing them 6 inches apart. When plants reach 4 to 6 inches tall, begin "dirting" them. This refers to mounding soil over the stems, leaving 2 inches of stem aboveground each time you add soil. Continue to add soil in this manner until the plant begins to flower. Potatoes should always be covered by soil, as sun will turn them green. Green potatoes contain toxins and shouldn't be consumed.

Fertilizing:
Fertilize at planting time with an organic, well-balanced, dry vegetable fertilizer. A month after planting, begin fertilizing with an organic tomato food every six weeks. Such a fertilizer will be low in nitrogen, which is important, as excessive nitrogen will lead to lush plants and little to no potatoes.

Watering:
Provide a consistent supply of even moisture. Overwatering leads to rotting potatoes, and droughting plants results in tough tubers.

Diseases:
Late Blight, Viruses, Verticillium Wilt. **Prevention:** Plant disease-free, certified seed potatoes or mini tubers that you get from a nursery or online seed provider. Remove and dispose of infected plants following harvest. Rotate crops.

Secret Growing Tip:
Grow bags, which are fabric bags designed for planting, are an ideal container for growing potatoes. They provide the perfect amount of aeration and drainage to support the formation of healthy tubers. Grow bags are also lightweight and easy to move around — a plus with heavy crops like potatoes.

Harvesting:
90 to 120 days after planting. When vines begin flowering, you can harvest "new" potatoes, which will be small, but delectable. Feel around in the soil and remove the new potatoes without disturbing the aboveground vine. Potatoes are ready for the final harvest when the foliage yellows and dies. Dig up the planting area with a trowel, being careful not to nick any of the potatoes. Then pull them out of the soil by hand.

Nutritional Nugget:
Potatoes are commonly seen as the "least healthy" vegetable because they're higher in starches and often fried or served with high-fat ingredients like sour cream and butter. But that doesn't mean they aren't nutritious! Potatoes are a good source of many vitamins and minerals, and colorful potatoes are also rich in antioxidants. Potatoes are naturally gluten-free — a great option for diets such as paleo.

Pumpkins

A staple of the fall season, pumpkins are a fun warm-season crop that appeals to the kid in everyone. This versatile member of the cucurbit family of plants that includes squash has many uses. Pumpkins make delicious pies, contain seeds that can be toasted into a yummy, nutritious treat, and are a popular Halloween decoration.

Pumpkins come in bush and vining types. Bush pumpkin varieties don't get as large as vining types, but they can still spread more than 20 feet. Vining pumpkins will roam more than 500 feet. Fruit size varies greatly with pumpkins and depends on the variety. Some cultivars grow giant, weighing 100 pounds or more, while others are small and have sweeter flesh, making them ideal for pies. Miniature varieties reach just 3 to 4 inches in size and are great fall decorations.

How to Grow a Giant Pumpkin:

If you wish to grow a giant pumpkin for Halloween, choose seeds for a cultivar known to grow large, such as 'Atlantic Giant' or 'Big Max'. Mix into the top 12 inches of soil a 6-inch-layer of compost. Then build a hill 18 inches wide by 6 inches tall. In early May, plant 4 to 6 seeds in the hill, 1 inch deep. Keep the hill moist while the seeds germinate and the seedlings begin growing. Once seedlings reach 4 inches tall, cut out all but the strongest seedling. Continue to keep the seedling moist and begin feeding monthly with a high nitrogen fertilizer, such as blood meal or feather meal. After the plant blossoms and fruits, allow several fruit to develop until they reach the size of a softball. At that time, choose the best one and cut off the others. Make the determination by looking for a pumpkin close to the roots with the thickest stem, best shape, color, and size. Continue to keep the soil moist and fertilize monthly. To give the plant even more energy to create a giant pumpkin, mound soil underneath the vine at 2-foot intervals. Roots will form at those points. Before the pumpkin gets too large to handle, slide a piece of plywood underneath the fruit. This will protect the bottom of the pumpkin from wet soil and resulting rot.

Growing Tips

Growing Season:
Spring - Fall

Container Growing Candidate:
No.

Location:
Full sun or afternoon shade. In the ground or raised bed. You must have a significant amount of space for the pumpkin vine to roam.

Soil:
Rich, well-draining soil. Mix into the top 12 inches of soil a 2- to 3-inch layer of compost. If the soil is particularly compacted, add pumice to improve drainage. Bulk up sandy soil with a 3- to 4-inch layer of compost.

Planting:
Plant pumpkin seeds outdoors in May and June, or start seed indoors in April for transplanting outdoors in May. When direct seeding in the garden, plant 3 to 4 seeds together 1 inch deep, 6 to 8 feet apart. When seedlings come up and reach 2 inches tall, cut out all but 1 plant in each grouping.

Fertilizing:
Fertilize at planting time with an organic, well-balanced, dry vegetable fertilizer. Once the plant begins growing, feed every 3 weeks with an organic, well-balanced, liquid fertilizer.

Watering:
Keep soil around pumpkin plants moist but not soggy. Avoid wetting foliage when watering to prevent foliar disease.

Diseases:
Sudden Wilt, Downy Mildew, Verticillium Wilt, Mosaic Virus. **Prevention:** Plant disease-resistant varieties. Rotate crops. Remove and destroy plant debris. Avoid wetting foliage when watering. Control weeds. Cover the soil in the planting area with aluminum foil to help reduce mosaic virus infections.

Secret Growing Tip:
If you'd like to monogram your pumpkin, scratch words or a symbol onto the fruit using the tip of a sharp knife or similar object. Do this in late August or early September before the shell has hardened. The inscription will callus over and become readable when the pumpkin matures.

Nutritional Nugget:
Like other orange vegetables, pumpkins are particularly rich in beta carotene, which the body converts to vitamin A. The fiber, potassium, and vitamin C in pumpkins supports heart health. Pumpkin seeds are a good source of the amino acid tryptophan, which along with the zinc and magnesium also found in pumpkins, helps promote good sleep.

Harvesting:
90 to 120 days after planting, depending on variety. Cut pumpkins from the vine when stems are hard and dry and the shell is hard.

Radishes

Spicy and crunchy, radishes make a refreshing addition to the cool-season garden. This easy-to-grow root vegetable is one of the quickest growing veggies for the home garden. Enjoy tasty radishes just 3 to 4 weeks after sowing seed.

Radishes come in a variety of colors and shapes. You'll find the roots in the standard red, as well as white and pink. Shapes include round, pointed, and cylindrical. Tastes also range from mild and sweet to super spicy.

Radishes grow best when temperatures are cool (50°F-70°F) and days are short. If temperatures are hot and days are long, the plant may not develop any roots, or the roots will be deformed and bitter. The plant will also quickly go to seed. Since radishes produce edible roots in just weeks, you can enjoy several crops throughout the cool season, if you do succession seeding.

Daikon Radishes:

If you eat Japanese cuisine, you've likely tasted daikon radishes. These long, white root vegetables contain a mustard-like oil that results in a spicy flavor. Daikons tend to be milder than many red radishes, though. You can ensure they are mild and juicy for you by growing them during SoCal's cool season. Except for in-ground soil preparation, daikon radishes require the same treatment as regular radishes. Since they are considerably longer than standard radishes, if you'll be growing daikons in the ground, they require deeper soil preparation. (Follow instructions for carrots.)

Growing Tips

Growing Season:
Fall - Spring

Container Growing Candidate:
Yes. Minimum 5-gallon container.

Location:
Light shade inland. Full sun along coast. Container or raised bed is best.

Soil:
Rich, well-draining soil that is easily worked. Southern California clay soil does not work well for radishes. Compacted, heavy soil leads to little to no radish growth. If you live in an area with sandy soil, such as along the coast, bulk up the soil with compost so that it is moisture retentive. If you wish to try growing in clay soil, add a 5- to 6-inch layer of compost and pumice to loosen up the soil down 8 to 10 inches.

Planting:
Sow radish seeds directly in the garden. Plant seeds 1/2 inch deep, 1 inch apart. Keep the soil moist at all times during germination. Radish seeds germinate in 4 to 5 days.

Fertilizing:
Fertilize with an organic, well-balanced, liquid fertilizer 10 days after planting. Since they are so fast-growing, radish plants only require the one feeding.

Watering:
Keep radish soil evenly moist but not soggy. Avoid letting the soil dry out, as this will lead to overly spicy, cracked radishes.

Diseases:
Downy Mildew. **Prevention:** Rotate crops. Remove plant debris promptly.

Secret Growing Tip:
Radishes can also be grown for their spicy leaves. Simply snip off leaves when they are 1 to 2 inches long and enjoy in salads. If you leave a small amount of green when snipping, the foliage will grow back.

Harvesting:
3 to 4 weeks after sowing seed. Harvest regularly when radishes are small and still tender. Wait too long to harvest and radishes become overly hot, spongy, and may be hollow inside.

Nutritional Nugget:
Radishes are known for their spicy bite, created when glucosinolates and the enzyme myrosinase combine when chewed to form allyl isothiocyanates (also present in mustard, horseradish, and wasabi). The bigger the radish and the warmer the weather when grown, the spicier. Radish greens often have a peppery taste like arugula and are a good source of vitamin C. Radish roots are rich in antioxidants and minerals like calcium and potassium.

Rutabagas

Members of the Brassica family, rutabagas originated as a cross between turnips and wild cabbage. Although often confused with turnips, this flavorful root vegetable has yellow flesh and a sweeter, milder, creamier taste. Rutabagas also grow more slowly and bigger than turnips.

Plant rutabagas in the fall and enjoy a healthy harvest of this tasty and nutritious root crop in the late winter and early spring. Rutabagas taste great in soups, stews, as a side dish, mashed, and as an accompaniment to poultry, beef or pork. Like turnips, the leaves of rutabaga can be eaten, but are only palatable when young and tender.

Nutritional Nugget:
Like all cruciferous vegetables, rutabagas are high in fiber. As a root vegetable, rutabagas are often used as a lower-carbohydrate and lower-calorie alternative to potatoes, especially for diabetic-friendly recipes (see keto-friendly fries recipe below). Vitamin C is the major vitamin in rutabagas, providing more than half our daily needs in a single serving.

Rutabaga Fries
Ingredients:
2 medium rutabagas, peeled and cut into spears
3-4 tablespoons olive oil (or avocado oil)
1 teaspoon paprika
1 teaspoon garlic powder
Salt and pepper to taste

Instructions:
Preheat oven to 425°F. Toss the rutabaga spears with oil and seasonings. Lay spears onto baking sheet. Bake for 30 minutes until crispy. Flip halfway through.

Growing Tips

Growing Season:
Fall - Spring

Container Growing Candidate:
Yes. Minimum 15-gallon container.

Location:
Full sun. Well-worked ground soil, container or raised bed.

Soil:
Rich, well-draining soil. Mix into the top 8 to 12 inches of clay soil a 3- to 4-inch layer of compost, if planting in the ground. Keep the growing area weed free.

Planting:
Sow rutabaga seeds directly in the garden in fall when the weather has cooled. Like many root crops, rutabaga doesn't transplant well. Plant seeds 1/4 to 1/2 inch deep, 1 inch apart. During germination, keep the soil moist at all times. When seedlings reach 2 to 3 inches tall, thin to 5 to 8 inches apart. It's important to provide rutabagas with enough growing room.

Fertilizing:
Fertilize at planting time with an organic, well-balanced, dry vegetable fertilizer. A month after planting, begin fertilizing monthly with an organic, well-balanced, liquid fertilizer.

Watering:
Keep rutabaga soil moist but not soggy. Avoid letting the soil dry out, as this can cause the root to become pungent in flavor. Mulch to preserve soil moisture and keep the roots cool.

Diseases:
Club Root. (Common in acidic soils).
Prevention: Increase air circulation. Plant disease-resistant varieties. Rotate crops.

Secret Growing Tip:
Rutabagas store well in the ground, where they can wait until you wish to harvest and use them. Dig them up by early spring.

Harvesting:
90 to 120 days after planting. Harvest when the root has grown 3 to 6 inches in diameter. Dig up with a garden fork and trim off roots and foliage.

Shallots

Favored in cooking for imparting a mild onion-garlic flavor to dishes, the young green shoots of this aromatic vegetable are also edible. You'll find two main types of shallots. These include Dutch varieties with golden-brown skin, and shallots featuring a red or purple skin.

Plant shallots in the fall, and you can enjoy their tasty greens throughout the winter and early spring. The bulbs will be ready for harvest in late spring or summer. Shallots are grown from cloves — small sections of a bulb. Each plant produces a cluster of several bulbs. If harvested correctly, you can store shallots in a cool, dry place for as long as 6 months.

Caramelized Shallots

Ingredients:
1 pound shallots (about 9-10)
2 tablespoons olive oil or butter
2 teaspoons brown sugar
Salt and pepper to taste

Instructions:
Clean and peel shallots; slice thinly. Heat oil (or butter) in a sauté pan over medium heat. Add the shallots and season with salt and pepper. Cook, stirring often, until the shallots soften and become translucent. Add brown sugar, then turn heat down to low and continue to cook until very soft and caramelized. This may take 15-30 more minutes.
Recipe variation: Add 3 Tbsp balsamic vinegar and 1 Tbsp brown sugar in addition to the brown sugar, above. Cook until sticky and soft.
Shallots can be used in pasta, pizzas, omelettes, sandwiches, or other recipes.
Store leftovers in the fridge for up to 5 days.

Nutritional Nugget:

Compared to their fellow onions, shallots have a lot to offer. This flavorful bulb provides a more concentrated source of protein, fiber, and micronutrients (magnesium, iron, phosphorus, potassium, folate, vitamin C, and B vitamins). Shallots are also packed with an array of antioxidants and organosulfur compounds that have antimicrobial properties.

Growing Tips

Growing Season:
Fall - Summer

Container Growing Candidate:
Yes. Minimum 10-gallon container.

Location:
Full sun. Container or raised bed is best.

Soil:
Rich, well-draining soil. Add a 2- to 3-inch layer of compost if planting in the ground in clay soil. Ensure that the planting area is free of any impediments, such as stones and sticks. Keep the growing area weed free.

Planting:
Plant shallot cloves with the enlarged base inserted into the soil facing downward and the tip just covered with soil. Space 4 to 8 inches apart.

Fertilizing:
Fertilize at planting time with an organic, well-balanced, dry vegetable fertilizer. In spring, begin applying an organic, well-balanced, liquid fertilizer monthly.

Watering:
Water shallots deeply but infrequently. If the soil stays too moist, the bulbs may rot. Water when the top 2 inches of soil have dried out. When the tops start to die back in the late spring or early summer indicating that harvest time is coming, pull back on watering.

Diseases:
Pink Root, White Rot, Purple Blotch. **Prevention:** Provide good air circulation. Rotate crops. Remove and destroy old plant vegetation. Avoid overwatering.

Secret Growing Tip:
Shallot cloves for planting can be purchased from the nursery or a seed company. Or simply separate grocery store shallots into cloves and plant them. Make sure to keep the skin intact when separating them.

Harvesting/Storage:
60 to 120 days after planting. Begin harvesting young green shoots at 60 days. Simply pinch or snip off the green tops, making sure to leave some green on each plant. The greens can be eaten raw or cooked. Bulbs will be ready for harvesting when the tops yellow and die. To harvest, gently pull up each plant and separate the bulbs from one another. Before using shallots, allow the outer skin to dry out completely for about a month. Lay harvested shallots in a basket to dry in a cool, dry place.

Sorrel

Revered for its distinctive lemony flavor in European cuisine, Sorrel makes a delicious addition to your year-round garden. This spinach-like green can be eaten raw or cooked, adding an intense flavor to soups, sauces, egg dishes, and salads. Sorrel pairs especially well with fish.

Three main types of sorrel exist. These are Broad Leaf, featuring slender, arrow-shaped leaves, French, with small, bell-shaped leaves and a mild flavor, and Red-Veined. As the latter sorrel's name suggests, its leaves feature bright red veins.

Plant sorrel in your garden once, and it will grow indefinitely for you. Sorrel is a perennial that will produce leaves all year. The plant is also heat tolerant and easy to grow, making it an ideal crop for any SoCal garden.

Sorrel Soup

Ingredients:
4 cups sorrel, rinsed and chopped
16 ounces chicken broth
1 tablespoon chives
2 teaspoons olive oil
3 tablespoons butter
1 cup nonfat or 1% milk
Pepper to taste

Instructions:
In olive oil, sauté sorrel in a skillet until tender. Add chicken broth. Simmer for 30-40 minutes until broth has taken on the flavor of the sorrel. Remove from heat. When cool, puree mixture in a food processor or with an immersion blender. Add remaining ingredients, except for chives, and bring to a rolling boil for 1 minute. Top with chives as desired and enjoy. Makes 2 to 4 servings.

Nutritional Nugget:

Sorrel has been used medicinally and in culinary preparations for centuries with a range of health benefits. Rich in fiber and vitamin C, and containing vitamin A, iron, magnesium, potassium, and calcium, sorrel is a nutrient-rich addition to your diet. Sorrel's additional beneficial organic compounds — polyphenolic acids, flavonoids, and anthocyanins — are all antioxidants that perform a lot of important functions in your body!

In the illustration above from left to right: French Sorrel, Broad Leaf Sorrel, Red-Veined Sorrel

Growing Tips

Growing Season:
Year-Round

Container Growing Candidate:
Yes. Minimum 5-gallon container for one plant.

Location:
Full sun. In the ground, raised bed or container.

Soil:
Rich, well-draining soil. Mix into the top 6 inches of clay soil a 2- to 3-inch layer of compost, if planting in the ground. Keep the area weed free.

Planting:
Seed directly in the garden or plant in containers and transplant when the seedlings are 3 to 4 inches tall. Sow seed 1/4 inch deep. When sowing directly, space 1 inch apart, thinning to 8 inches apart when the plants reach 2 inches tall. Plant transplants 8 inches apart.

Fertilizing:
Fertilize at planting time with an organic, well-balanced, dry vegetable fertilizer. When plants reach 4 to 5 inches tall, water with an organic, well-balanced, liquid fertilizer every 2 to 3 months.

Watering:
Keep the soil around sorrel plants moist but not soggy. Because sorrel is a leafy green, it's important not to let the soil dry out.

Diseases:
None of note.

Secret Growing Tip:
Sorrel will reseed itself in fertile soil. This will ensure that you have an abundant, continuous crop for years.

Harvesting:
60 days after sowing seed or when the leaves are large enough to eat. Snap or cut each leaf off at the base of the plant.

Spinach

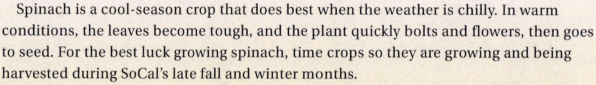

If you like eating fresh spinach, you're sure to enjoy harvesting this nutritious green from your home garden. Homegrown spinach is delicious raw and cooked in dishes like stir-fries and quiches.

Spinach is a cool-season crop that does best when the weather is chilly. In warm conditions, the leaves become tough, and the plant quickly bolts and flowers, then goes to seed. For the best luck growing spinach, time crops so they are growing and being harvested during SoCal's late fall and winter months.

Quick to grow from seed, spinach produces edible leaves in just 40 to 50 days. That means you can plant and enjoy two or three crops during the cool season. Planting more than one crop also gives you a backup should the weather turn unseasonably warm and cause a crop to go to seed.

New Zealand Spinach:

While not a true spinach, New Zealand spinach resembles regular spinach in leaf shape and taste, although the leaves are a bit tougher. Gardeners often choose to grow this plant instead of standard spinach, because New Zealand spinach does a much better job of standing up to SoCal's drought and heat. Use New Zealand spinach as you would regular spinach. It can be cooked or used raw in salads. The plant also has the same growing requirements as standard spinach.

Growing Tips

Growing Season:
Fall - Early Spring
(Year-Round along Coast)

Container Growing Candidate:
Yes. Minimum 10-gallon container.

Location:
Full sun.

Soil:
Rich, well-draining soil. If planting in the ground, loosen clay soil by mixing in a 3-inch layer of compost into the top 8 inches of soil. Bulk up sandy soil by mixing in a 4-inch layer of compost into the top 8 inches of soil. Keep growing area weed free.

Planting:
Seed directly in the garden. Sow seed 1/2 inch deep, 1 inch apart. When seedlings reach 2 inches tall, thin to 3 to 4 inches apart.

Fertilizing:
Fertilize at planting time with an organic, well-balanced, dry vegetable fertilizer. A month after planting, begin fertilizing monthly with an organic, well-balanced, liquid fertilizer.

Watering:
Keep spinach soil consistently moist but not soggy. Fluctuations in soil moisture levels can cause spinach to bolt and go to seed. Mulch to preserve soil moisture and keep the roots cool.

Diseases:
Downy Mildew. **Prevention:** Plant disease-resistant varieties. Provide good air circulation. Plant in well-draining soil. Rotate crops. Remove and destroy old vegetation. Avoid overwatering.

Secret Growing Tip:
Breeders have worked for years to develop spinach cultivars that are slow to bolt. Increase your odds of growing a successful crop of spinach by choosing a slow bolting variety.

Harvesting:
40 to 50 days after planting. Spinach is ready to harvest when the plant has produced 6 to 8 leaves. Remove just the outer leaves as needed, or cut the entire plant. Leave 2 inches of growth at the base of the plant when harvesting the whole plant. It will regrow.

Nutritional Nugget:
Three cups of raw spinach contain 300% of the daily need for bone-supporting vitamin K, 160% of the daily need for vitamin A, and about 45% of the daily need for folate, a B vitamin that helps form red blood cells and DNA. Spinach is also packed with various phytonutrients, including the carotenoids lutein and zeaxanthin, known for their impact on vision health! The fiber in spinach is mostly insoluble fiber, the kind that helps with digestive health.

Sprouts

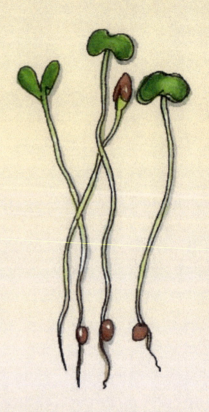

Packed with nutrients and flavor, sprouts are an easy vegetable crop that you can grow in your kitchen. Even better, these flavorful sprouted seeds are quick-growing. You can plant sprouts and harvest in less than a week.

Unlike many vegetable crops that require soil and sun, sprouts, which are germinated seeds, only need water and the right temperature, which is 65°F-75°F. You can sprout a wide variety of dried seeds, beans, and grains. Enjoy alfalfa, cress, chia, clover, mustard, lentil, green pea, garbanzo bean, fenugreek, broccoli, mung bean, adzuki, onion, radish, sesame, soybean, and more. Enjoy sprouts in salads, soups, sandwiches, stir-fries, and baked into casseroles and breads.

Three-Tiered Sprouter Tray

Nutritional Nugget:

Sprouts are often regarded as nutritional powerhouses with numerous nutrients packed into their small size. While the vitamins, minerals, and beneficial plant compounds contained vary based on variety, generally speaking sprouts are rich in vitamin K, vitamin C, and multiple B vitamins. The process of sprouting can help increase nutrient bioavailability, including protein, and aid in digestibility through reduction of antinutrients, which interfere with nutrient absorption in the body.

Growing Tips

Growing Season:
Year-Round

Container Growing Candidate:
Yes, indoors.

Location:
Out of direct sunlight in your kitchen.

Soil:
Sprouts need a sterile vessel in which to sprout; no soil is required. That can be a sprouting jar, such as a mason jar with a screen lid, or a sprouter designed to grow sprouts. Sprouters are generally tiered systems that allow for sprouting several types at once. These systems provide sprouts sufficient space to grow and good air circulation.

Planting:
Use seeds for sprouting, not planting. The amount of seed you use will depend on the size of the sprouter. For a quart jar, add 1 to 3 tablespoons of seed, depending on the size of the seed.

Fertilizing:
None required.

Watering:
Sprouts grow in moisture, but not standing water. They need to be kept moist through regular rinsing, which keeps them hydrated and fresh. If sprouts dry out at any point, they will stop sprouting. Rinse sprouts with water 2 to 3 times a day during germination and growth. Seed sprouting units are designed to rinse in place. You simply add water at the top of the unit, and it filters through to the bottom. Carefully empty the water from the bottom tray. Mason jars are easy to rinse. You simply pour water through the screen top and then turn the bottle over and drain, making sure not to lose any seeds.

Diseases:
Since sprouts grow quickly, they will not be impacted by diseases, but they can become contaminated with harmful bacteria such as e. coli and salmonella. With this in mind, it is important to follow safe food handling practices when sprouting at home. Purchase only high-quality sprouting seeds that have been tested for these bacteria, and prior to use, always wash your sprouter with warm, sudsy water and rinse in hot water prior to filling with seeds. Mason jars can be sterilized in the dishwasher. Avoid touching the seeds or sprouts with your hands. Use a spoon to place the seeds in the sprouter and tongs to harvest the sprouts. Always clean the sprouter between uses.

Prevent mold and fruit flies. Both of these problems can be solved by lowering the temperature in the room where the sprouts are growing, as well as using less seed so that the sprouts have sufficient air circulation. Creating air movement with a fan also keeps mold and fruit flies away. Sprouts grow best at 65°F.

Secret Growing Tip:
Once the sprouts are ready to eat, place them in indirect, bright light for a few hours. This will green them up.

Harvesting:
Within 3 to 7 days. Eat as soon as possible after harvesting. Sprouts can be stored up to 3 days in the refrigerator in a container lined with paper towels to soak up moisture.

Squash

Few vegetables are as easy to grow as squash. It's a rewarding crop for newbie gardeners, and just as fulfilling for experienced green thumbs. This is especially the case if you grow a variety of squash.

Many gardeners think of zucchini when it comes to planting squash in the garden, but there are a plethora of options to consider. Within the two main categories of squash — summer and winter — you'll find many tasty options. You'll also find bush and vining varieties of squash. Bush types take up less space in the garden.

The difference between summer and winter squash has to do with the stage at which the squash is harvested. Summer squash, such as zucchini and crookneck, is picked and eaten during warm weather. Winter squash, such as acorn and butternut, is harvested in the fall and can be stored for several months.

Whereas the skin of summer squash is thin and edible, and the entire vegetable can be eaten raw or cooked, winter squash skin is hard and inedible. You need to cook the interior of the vegetable before consuming it. The hard outer shell of winter squash allows for storing the vegetable up to 4 months.

Spiralized Zucchini Noodles with Shrimp

Nutritional Nugget:
Most varieties of squash are high in vitamin C, which in addition to supporting immune health, aids in collagen formation essential to maintaining healthy bones, skin, and teeth. The antioxidants in squash vary based on the plant pigments of each type of squash, but all provide varying health benefits. The highest levels of antioxidants are contained in squash skin.

Growing Tips

Growing Season:
Spring - Fall

Container Growing Candidate:
Yes. Minimum 15 gallon container. Choose small squash varieties, such as patty pan.

Location:
Full sun. In the ground or raised bed is best, as squash needs considerable room for root and foliage development.

Soil:
Rich, well-draining soil. Mix into the top 12 inches of soil a 3- to 4-inch layer of compost. If the soil is particularly compacted, add pumice to improve drainage. Bulk up sandy soil with a 3- to 4-inch layer of compost.

Planting:
Plant squash seeds outdoors throughout the spring and early summer, or start seed indoors in March for transplanting outdoors starting in April. When direct seeding in the garden, sow seeds for vining squash 2 inches deep, 6 inches apart. Once the seedlings reach 2 inches tall, thin to 5 to 8 feet apart. Sow seeds of bush squash 2 inches deep, 4 inches apart. Thin seedlings to 2 to 4 feet apart.

Fertilizing:
Fertilize at planting time with an organic, well-balanced, dry vegetable fertilizer. A month after planting, begin feeding every 3 weeks with an organic, well-balanced, liquid fertilizer.

Watering:
Keep soil around squash plants moist but not soggy. Ensure consistent, even watering when fruit is forming. Avoid wetting foliage and stems during irrigation to prevent foliar disease.

Diseases:
Downy Mildew, Powdery Mildew, Leaf Spot. Fusarium Wilt.
Prevention: Plant disease-resistant varieties. Rotate crops. Remove and destroy infected plants. Avoid wetting foliage when watering. Control weeds. Dust with sulfur for Powdery Mildew.

Secret Growing Tip:
If you find that your squash plant isn't forming fruit, it may be a lack of pollination from bees. (Squash pollen is sticky, so wind can't pollinate these plants.) To ensure pollination and fruit set, hand pollination between male and female flowers may be necessary. Female flowers contain a miniature fruit within the flower. Male flowers have no fruit, but instead contain yellow pollen. To pollinate, use a small paintbrush or a male flower. If using a flower, remove the petals to expose the pollen-bearing area. Roll the pollen onto the stigma in the female flower. Only use squash flowers that opened within the last 24 hours, as that is how long the pollen is viable.

Harvesting:
50 to 65 days after planting for summer squash. 60 to 110 days after planting for winter squash. Harvest summer squash when the fruit is small and the skins are still tender and can easily be punctured with your fingernail. Avoid waiting until the squash gets large and the skin becomes hardened. At that point, the squash will lose flavor and become watery, and the plant will stop producing. Cut the squash off the plant with a sharp knife. Harvest winter squash when skins are thoroughly hardened and not scratchable. Cut off with an inch of stem and store in a cool, dry place until ready to use.

Swiss Chard

Often simply referred to as chard, Swiss chard is a form of beet grown for its leaves and stalks, rather than its roots. The leafy vegetable is easy to grow and adds a colorful addition to the garden. Chard produces an abundance of eye-catching edible leaves fall through spring inland and year-round along the coast.

Swiss chard's leaves come in a variety of stunning color combinations. These include green foliage with white, pink, yellow, orange, or red veins and stems. Chard leaves can be eaten raw in salads and on sandwiches or cooked in stir-fries, soups, quiches, casseroles, and more.

Bacon & Swiss Chard Quiche

Ingredients:
1 large bunch Swiss chard, chopped in 1-inch pieces
1 10-inch pie crust, unbaked
1/2 pound Monterey jack cheese, grated
4 eggs
2 tablespoons flour
3/4 cup milk
8 slices bacon
1/2 medium onion, finely chopped
Salt and pepper to taste

Instructions:
Preheat oven to 350°F. Cook bacon in a skillet until crispy and browned; set aside to let cool and then crumble into smaller pieces. Add onions to pan with remaining bacon grease and cook over medium heat until soft and brown, about 8 minutes. Place Swiss chard in the pie shell. Sprinkle cheese evenly over the greens. Mix eggs, flour, milk, crumbled bacon, onion, salt, and pepper in a medium bowl and pour over cheese. Bake for 45-55 minutes or until golden brown and a knife inserted comes out clean. Let cool 10 minutes before serving. Makes 6 to 8 servings.

Growing Tips

Growing Season:
Fall - Spring (Year-Round along Coast)

Container Growing Candidate:
Yes. Minimum 10-gallon container.

Location:
Full sun or partial shade.

Soil:
Rich, well-draining soil. If planting in the ground, loosen clay soil by mixing in a 3-inch layer of compost into the top 6 inches of soil. Bulk up sandy soil by mixing in a 4-inch layer of compost into the top 6 inches of soil.

Planting:
Seed directly in the garden or plant in containers and transplant when the seedlings are 2 to 4 inches tall. Sow seed 1/4 to 1/2 inch deep. When sowing directly, space seed 3 inches apart, thinning to 12 inches apart when the plants reach 2 to 3 inches tall. Plant transplants 12 inches apart. Chard requires room to grow, as the plant can reach up to 2 feet tall and 18 inches wide.

Fertilizing:
Fertilize at planting time with an organic, well-balanced, dry vegetable fertilizer. A month after planting, begin fertilizing monthly with an organic, well-balanced, liquid fertilizer.

Watering:
Water Swiss chard when the soil surface is approaching dryness. Once chard becomes established, the plant can withstand some drought. However, for the most succulent leaves possible, maintain a regular watering schedule.

Diseases:
Curly Top Virus. **Prevention:** Avoid growing in hot weather when chard is most susceptible to the disease. Spread by beet leafhoppers that thrive in weeds — so control weeds.

Secret Growing Tip:
The striking stems and leaves of Swiss chard make a colorful addition to cut floral arrangements. To increase vase life, cut chard stems at an angle and insert into warm water immediately.

Nutritional Nugget:
Swiss chard, like other dark leafy greens, is one of the richest vegetable sources of vitamin K, with more than 3 times the daily recommended amount per 1 cup serving! The leafy green is also an excellent source of vitamin A, vitamin C, magnesium, manganese, iron, and potassium. Swiss chard is high in fiber and antioxidants, which help to regulate blood sugar levels and promote healthy digestion.

Harvesting:
50 to 60 days after planting. Swiss chard is quick to produce edible leaves. Harvest individual leaves as you need them, making sure not to cut too close to the plant. Pick outer leaves first, as they become stringy and tough when left on the plant. You can also cut the whole plant for use. Leave 2 inches of stem when harvesting the entire plant. It will resprout and grow more leaves. Stalks take much longer to become tender than leaves, so cook separately. For eating raw in salads and on sandwiches, harvest leaves when young and tender at no more than 2 inches in length.

Tomatillos

As their name suggests, tomatillos are tomato relatives. Heat-lovers that thrive in low humidity, tomatillos are an ideal crop for the SoCal warm-season garden. Resembling green tomatoes with a husk, tomatillos are easy to grow. The plants have a rambling, sprawling growth habit and will reach 3 to 4 feet tall. For healthy growth, they require staking or trellising when plants are young.

In ideal growing conditions, one tomatillo plant can grow as much as 10 pounds of fruit in a season. This is good news if you enjoy salsa verde and wish to make your own. In addition to salsa, tomatillos can be used raw in salads or diced and cooked in stews, sauces, and moles.

Tomatillos are not self-pollinating. It is important to plant at least two plants within 2 to 3 few feet of one another in order to get a good-sized crop. Bees swarm to the plant's pretty yellow flowers and will do the pollinating for you. Wind will also pollinate tomatillos.

Easy Tomatillo Salsa Verde

Ingredients:
1 pound fresh tomatillos, husks removed & rinsed
1 serrano pepper (or 2 jalapeño peppers), stem & seeds removed
1 small white onion, chopped
1/2 cup fresh cilantro leaves
2 cloves (or more) garlic *(optional)*
1 tablespoon lime juice
Salt to taste

Instructions:
Preheat oven to 425°F. Spread tomatillos and peppers on a large baking sheet lined with foil. Roast in the oven for 15 minutes, or until the tomatillos start to brown on top and are cooked through. Remove from oven and transfer to a blender or food processor. Add the onion, cilantro, garlic, lime juice, and salt to the blender or food processor, and pulse until it reaches desired consistency. Season with extra salt or cilantro to taste. Salsa can be refrigerated for up to 5 days. Makes 16 oz of salsa.

Nutritional Nugget:
Tomatillos, while small in size, are packed with vitamin C, vitamin K, and several minerals, including copper and iron. Each tomatillo boasts about 1 gram of fiber, an important ingredient of a heart-healthy diet! Tomatillos also contain lutein and zeaxanthin — carotenoids that boost eye health.

Growing Tips

Growing Season:
Spring-Summer

Container Growing Candidate:
Yes. Minimum 15-gallon container for one plant.

Location:
Full sun (minimum 8 hours). Area with good air circulation and adequate growing room.

Soil:
Rich, well-draining soil. Improve drainage in clay soil by amending with a 2- to 3-inch layer of compost. Add 1 cup of pumice to each planting hole in especially heavy soil. Bulk up sandy soil by adding a 3- to 4-inch layer of compost.

Planting:
Seed directly in the garden or plant in containers and transplant when the seedlings are 2 to 3 inches tall. Sow seed 1/8 inch deep, 2 inches apart. Seeds germinate in about 5 days in warm, moist soil. Thin seedlings to 10 to 12 inches apart once they reach 2 to 3 inches tall. Install growing supports at planting time, as tomatillos grow quickly. When planting transplants, bury the stem just under the bottom set of leaves. Doing this will encourage healthy rooting.

Fertilizing:
Feed monthly with an organic tomato food once the plant is at least 6 inches tall. Such a fertilizer will be low in nitrogen, which is important, as excessive nitrogen will lead to lush tomatillo plants and no fruit.

Watering:
When plants are young, keep the soil moist but not soggy. Once they reach 6 to 8 inches tall and have become established, only water when the first 2 to 3 inches of soil have dried. This could be every 5 to 10 days. Pull back even more on watering when plants flower and fruit starts to form. Avoid letting the plant get water stressed, though.

Diseases:
Black Spot, Verticillium Wilt, Fusarium Wilt, Powdery Mildew. **Prevention:** Plant disease-resistant varieties. Such plants are indicated by a V for Verticillium. Remove and dispose of infected plants following harvest. Rotate crops. Avoid watering and wetting foliage later in the day.

Secret Growing Tip:
Though more rare, tomatillos also come in a beautiful purple variety. They are a bit smaller than green tomatillos and have a much sweeter, citrusy taste compared to their green counterparts. Many gardeners like to eat the purple tomatillos right off the vine. The more sunshine the purple variety receives, the sweeter the flavor.

Harvesting/Storage:
120 days after planting. Harvest when the tomatillos are about the size of a walnut or slightly smaller and deep green in color. The papery husks around them will have turned tan and started to split. Don't remove the husks until you're ready to use the fruit.

Tomatoes

The adage "nothing like homegrown" certainly came from experiencing a garden-ripe tomato. Tomatoes are one of the most popular of all home garden crops, and for good reason. The enticing taste of a homegrown tomato — with just the right mix of acidic and sweet — is unparalleled when it comes to growing your own.

SoCal has the ideal climate for growing tomatoes throughout the year. While you generally won't get an overflowing crop in the cold winter months, you can still get tomatoes. (See Chapter 1 for winter growing instructions).

Tomatoes are a bit on the precocious side. They may grow like weeds one year and the next year decide not to cooperate. That has to do with a variety of conditions, including the location where you plant them and the weather.

Nowadays, you can grow just about any type of tomato you choose. Oodles of heirloom varieties exist in enticing colors, including purple, "black" (actually a very dark purple), green, marbleized, pink, and many shades of red. The flavor variations are astounding, as well. The many hybrid varieties are dependable, prolific, and equally as tasty. Sizes run the gamut, from 'Tom Thumb' itty-bitty tomatoes to giant beefsteak varieties that can feed three people. Shopping for tomato varieties offers you a smorgasbord of delectable choices.

Tomatoes come in determinate and indeterminate varieties. Generally, determinate tomatoes are bush types that stop growing when they reach 3 to 4 feet tall. Their crops ripen over a shorter period than indeterminate. The latter tomato type keeps growing indefinitely, with the plants reaching 12 to 14 feet in height. Indeterminate varieties are best for winter growing.

Nutritional Nugget:

The tomato's bright red color comes from lycopene, a carotenoid known for its numerous health benefits. Pair your tomato with olive oil to raise its antioxidant activity!

Growing Tips

Growing Season:
Year-Round

Container Growing Candidate:
Yes. Minimum 15-gallon container for one plant. Choose small to medium-sized tomatoes.

Location:
Full sun (minimum 8 hours). Area with good air circulation and adequate growing room.

Soil:
Rich, well-draining soil. Improve drainage in clay soil by amending with a 2- to 3-inch layer of compost. Add 1 cup of pumice to each planting hole in especially heavy soil. Bulk up sandy soil by adding a 3- to 4-inch layer of compost.

Planting:
Plant transplants 4 to 5 feet apart. Indeterminate tomatoes need strong support, so use sturdy, large cages reinforced with stakes. Determinate tomatoes generally grow well in standard tomato cages. Tomatoes are deep-rooted and for that reason need to be planted deep. Pinch off the bottom one to five leaves at the stem, making sure to leave at least one set of leaves at the top. Bury the stem in soil to just above the last notch left from leaf removal. Roots will emerge from the notches, creating a stronger plant. (See Chapter 1 for a how-to illustration).

Fertilizing:
Feed with an organic tomato food once the plant is at least 6 inches tall. Such a fertilizer will be low in nitrogen, which is important, as excessive nitrogen will lead to lush plants and no fruit.

Watering:
Water established plants when the first 3 to 4 inches of soil have dried. Overwatering leads to watery fruit and disease. Tomatoes slightly stressed from minor underwatering are more likely to shift into production mode, triggering blooming and fruiting. Newly transplanted tomatoes will require watering every day, then every other day; tapering off on watering until the plant becomes established.

Diseases:
Leaf Spot, Verticillium Wilt, Fusarium Wilt, Gray Mold, Anthracnose, Blight, Blossom End Rot, Cracking.
Prevention: Plant disease-resistant varieties. Such plants are indicated by a V for Verticillium. Maintain a fertilizing regimen. Remove and dispose of infected plants following harvest. Rotate crops. Provide adequate air circulation. Avoid overwatering.

Secret Growing Tip:
Use a blossom set spray, which contains a natural plant hormone that can stimulate tomato plants to flower and set fruit, even when weather conditions aren't ideal. (When temperatures surpass 90°F in the day and 75°F at night for an extended period of time, tomatoes generally stop setting fruit, because pollen becomes unviable).

Harvesting:
35 to 120 days after planting, depending on variety. Harvest fruit when the color is deep and the tomato gives slightly when squeezed.

Turnips

Grown for their leafy tops and enlarged roots, turnips are a member of the Brassica family of plants. This fast-growing root crop features a bold flavor and makes an excellent addition to your cool-season garden.

Turnips are white, white with a purple top, and creamy yellow. With most turnip varieties, you can eat the tops and roots, but there are some types that you grow exclusively for the leaves (turnip greens). Steam the leaves and season with butter or olive oil. The turnip root can be eaten raw or cooked. For an especially tasty treat, try pickled turnips.

Nutritional Nugget:
While turnip roots are a flavorful low-calorie veggie filled with vitamins and minerals, turnip greens pack an even greater nutritional punch! Both turnip roots and greens provide more than 30% of the daily value of vitamin C per serving. The greens are an excellent source of vitamin K, provitamin A (beta carotene), and folate. As a non-starchy vegetable, turnips are another great option low on the glycemic index.

Beetroot Pickled Turnips

Ingredients:
2 turnips (about 1 lb), peeled and cut into 1/4-inch spears
1 small red beet, peeled and quartered
1 clove garlic, sliced
1/2 cup white vinegar
2 tablespoons Kosher salt + 1 teaspoon sugar
1 1/2 cups (12 oz) water
1 bay leaf *(optional)*

Instructions:
Place turnips, beet, and garlic in a wide-mouth 1-quart glass jar. In a medium pot, bring vinegar, salt, sugar, and water to a boil. Once sugar and salt are dissolved, pour the brine over the veggies to fill the jar. Leave to cool, then cover the jar and chill in fridge for at least 1 day.

Growing Tips

Growing Season:
Fall - Spring

Container Growing Candidate:
Yes. Minimum 15-gallon container.

Location:
Full sun. Well-worked ground soil, container or raised bed.

Soil:
Rich, well-draining soil. Mix into the top 6 to 10 inches of clay soil a 3- to 4-inch layer of compost, if planting in the ground. Keep the growing area weed free.

Planting:
Sow turnip seed directly in the garden in fall when the weather has cooled. Like other root crops, turnips don't transplant well. Plant seeds 1/4 to 1/2 inch deep, 1 inch apart. During germination, keep the soil moist at all times. When seedlings reach 2 to 3 inches tall, thin to 5 to 8 inches apart.

Fertilizing:
Fertilize at planting time with an organic, well-balanced, dry vegetable fertilizer. A month after planting, begin fertilizing monthly with an organic, well-balanced, liquid fertilizer.

Watering:
Keep turnip soil moist but not soggy. Avoid letting the soil dry out, as this can cause the root to split or the plant to bolt (flower and go to seed). Mulch to preserve soil moisture and keep the roots cool.

Diseases:
Downy Mildew. **Prevention:** Immediately remove and dispose of infected plants. Rotate crops. Don't overcrowd plants.

Secret Growing Tip:
If you only wish to grow turnips for their tasty leaves, you can plant them close together at 1 to 3 inches apart.

Harvesting:
35 to 75 days after planting. Harvest turnips when they are the size of a golf ball and no larger than a small orange. If left in the soil any longer, they will become woody and tasteless. Dig up with a garden fork and trim off roots and foliage. Harvest turnip greens for cooking when they reach about 6 inches long. Cut them off with scissors. If you are also growing the turnip for roots, don't harvest all of the leaves.

About the Authors

Julie Bawden-Davis is a Southern California bestselling garden author, instructor, and master gardener, who began developing her green thumb when she started writing at an early age. A former gardening columnist for the *Los Angeles Times* and Parade.com, Julie is author of several gardening books, including *The Strawberry Story: How To Grow Great Berries Year-Round in Southern California*, *Fairy Gardening: Creating Your Own Magical Miniature Garden*, *Indoor Gardening the Organic Way*, and co-author of *Southern California Vegetable Gardening* and *Southern California Fruit Gardening* (SoCal Year-Round Gardening Series). She is also founder and publisher of HealthyHouseplants.com and a member of Garden Communicators International. Julie teaches classes about growing and enjoying homegrown produce in her "From the Garden to the Kitchen" series. She gains inspiration from puttering, planting, and pruning in her SoCal garden, certified in 1999 by the National Wildlife Federation as a Backyard Wildlife Habitat.

Sabrina Wildermuth is a food scientist, whose love for food and its fascinating chemical properties all started in the garden. With the help of her mom, she started gardening at the age of 2, planting sunflowers that towered over her and tomatoes she ate like apples out in the garden. In college, Sabrina conducted impactful research on the reaction of an antioxidant, chlorogenic acid, with the proteins in sunflower butter to determine why it turns cookies bright green. For the last decade, she has had a rewarding career in the food and supplements industries focusing on nutrition labeling, new product development, and regulatory compliance and product safety. Sabrina spends her free time with her husband and son growing a bounty of produce in raised beds in their Southern California garden. She is the co-author of *Southern California Vegetable Gardening* and *Southern California Fruit Gardening* (SoCal Year-Round Gardening Series).

Books in the SoCal Year-Round Gardening Series

Southern California Vegetable Gardening
Southern California Fruit Gardening
Southern California Herb Gardening (Coming soon!)

Your Opinion Matters!

If you liked this book, please leave a review on Amazon, GoodReads, BookBub, or all three. If you don't wish to leave a review, or don't have time, please leave a rating. Every star helps!

Index

A
Alfalfa Meal 16, 22
All America Selections (AAA) 33
Angular Leaf Spot 41, 76
Anti-transpirant 6
Aphids 31-34, 36-39, 74
Artichokes 11, 51-52
Arugula 53-54
Asparagus 55-56
Aster Yellows 41, 72

B
Bacillus amyloliquefaciens 41
Bacillus thuringiensis 38
Bacterial Leaf Spot 41, 54
Bagrada bug 34
Beans 57-58
Beetles (Cucumber, Colorado potato), 32, 34, 36, 38
Beets 11, 23, 25, 28, 59-60
Birds 31-32, 34-35, 43
Blight 41, 96, 102, 124
Bloodmeal 16, 22
Blossom End Rot 18, 41, 124
Bolting 4, 61, 80, 92, 114
Bonemeal 16, 22, 56
Botrytis Fungus 41, 52, 56
Brassica family of plants 6, 33, 61, 63, 65, 69, 82, 83, 85, 107, 125
Broccoli 61-63, 115
Broccolini / Broccoli Rabe 61
Brussels Sprouts ii, 12, 26, 61, 63-64

C
Cabbage 6, 65-66, 85
Cabbage Butterfly (caterpillar) 33
Cabbage Root Maggot 34
Calcium
  in soil and vegetables 18, 21-22, 106, 111
  and gypsum 18
  deficiency and blossom end rot 18
Carrots ii, 11, 23, 28-29, 59, 67-68, 93, 105
Caterpillars (Cabbage Moth/Loopers) 33-34, 38
Cauliflower 4, 6, 26, 32, 61, 63, 69-70
Celeriac 71
Celery 71-72
Chard (*see Swiss Chard*)
Chicken manure 15, 22, 56
Children (gardening with) 43-47
Climate change 1
Club Root 41, 66, 70, 86, 108

Coastal gardening 8, 11-14, 51-52, 54, 60, 63, 65-66, 68, 82, 90, 94, 102, 106, 114, 119-120
Coir (coconut) 16-17
Collards 83
Companion planting 36
Composting 14-15, 17
Containers/pots
  and water conservation 1
  drainage 6
  for small space 2
  growing in 1, 10, 20, 47, 50
  pH 19
  protecting from frost 6-7
  soil for 15-16
Corn 73-74
Corn earworms 34, 39
Cottonseed meal 22
Cucamelons 43, 75
Cucumbers 75-76
Curly Dwarf Virus/Curly Top Virus 41, 52, 60, 120
Cutworms 34-35, 39
Crown Rot 41, 52, 56, 72

D
Damping Off 41
Diatomaceous Earth 39
Diseases 32-33
Disease-resistant 18, 33, 40, 62, 64, 70, 74, 78, 84, 88, 90, 92, 98, 104, 108, 114, 118, 122, 124
Downy Mildew 11, 41, 54, 62, 64, 70, 80, 88, 90, 92, 98, 104, 106, 114, 118, 126
Drainage (*see soil, drainage*)
Drought 1-3

E
EPA 1
Epsom salts 22
Eggplant 77-78

F
Feather Meal 16, 22, 56, 103
Fertilizing
  benefits of organic 19-20
  choosing organic fertilizer 21
  dangers of synthetic fertilizer 19-20
  how to apply 20
  types of organic fertilizer 20
Fish Emulsion 22
Fish Meal 16, 22
Frost/freezing
  damage 6
  frost blanket 7
  protecting plants from 6-7
Fungal diseases i, 10, 41, 90
Fungal Leaf Spot 41, 72
Fusarium Root Rot 41, 58
Fusarium Wilt 41, 55-56, 84, 98, 118, 122, 124

G
Garlic 79-80
GMO 25
Gophers 34-35
Grasshoppers 34-35, 40
Gray Mold 41, 124
Greens for stir-fry 81-82
Greensand 22
Growing out of season
   winter tomatoes 6-10
Guano (bat, bird) 16, 22
Gypsum 18, 22

H
Horticultural oil 39
Humidity 2, 4, 69, 121
Humus/humic acid 16-17, 22

I
Insecticidal soap sprays 39
Iron 21, 22, 40, 59, 81, 89, 95, 109, 111, 120, 121
Isopropyl alcohol 39

J
June Gloom i, 11

K
Kale 6, 23, 61, 82-84
Kelp Meal 22
Kohlrabi 85-86

L
Ladybird beetle/ladybug 32, 37
Langbeinite 22, 76
Leaf Blight 41, 68
Leaf Spot 11
Leafhoppers 34, 41, 60, 72, 120
Leafminers 34, 40
Leeks 28, 87-88
Lettuce 11, 23-24, 28, 89-90

M
Magnesium 18, 21-22, 51, 74, 76, 81, 95, 100, 104, 109, 111, 120
Marigolds 36-37
Mediterranean climate i, 50-51, 54
Microclimates 7-8
Mosaic Virus 41, 74, 78, 100, 104
Mulching
   and erosion control 6
   and water conservation 1-2
   and watering 17
   and winter tomatoes 10
   benefits of 16-17
   types of 2
Mycorrhizae 17-18

N
Neem oil 39
Nematodes 34, 36, 38
Nitric acid 5
Nitrogen 10, 15, 18, 21-22, 56, 58, 74, 76, 86, 90, 98, 102-103, 122, 124
Nitrogen-fixing bacteria 58, 98
N-P-K 21

O
Onions 28, 91-92, 109, 119
   green onions 91
Oyster shells 22

P
Parsnips 28, 93-94
Peanuts 19, 28, 95-96
Peas 24, 30, 47, 58, 97-98
Peat moss 16
Peppers 6, 99-100, 121
Perlite 14, 16
Pests
   about 31
   beneficial insects 31-32
   exotic, invasive pests 31
   identification 34
   organic pest control 34-41
pH (*see soil pH/checking*)
Phosphorus 18, 21-22, 51, 95, 109
Photosynthesis 18, 45
Pink Root 41, 80, 92, 110
Popcorn 73
Possums 34-35
Potassium 21-22, 51, 71, 76, 81, 85, 95, 99, 101, 104, 106, 109, 111, 120
Potatoes 101-102, 107
Pots (see containers)
Powdery Mildew 11, 32, 41, 68, 76, 98, 118, 122
Propagating 23-30
Pumice 14, 16
Pumpkins 28, 103-104
Purple Blotch 41, 88, 110
Pyrethrins 40

R
Rabbits 31, 34-35
Raccoons 34-35
Radishes 28, 47, 105-106
   Daikon 105
Rain
   barrels 3
   benefits of 5
   collecting, 2-3
   lack of i
   flooding 5-6
Raised beds 1, 15
Rock phosphate 22
Roots (*see soil*)
Root Rot 5, 10, 17, 41, 58, 66, 86
Rotating crops 37
Rutabagas 28, 107-108

Index

S
Santa Ana Winds (*see windy weather*)
Seaweed 22
Seeding
  benefits of 23
  direct sowing 28-29
  GMO (none) 25
  hardening off seedlings 27
  harvesting seeds 30
  hybrid seeds 23-25
  indoor seeding 25-26
  open pollinated seeds 23, 25, 30
  storage and longevity of seeds 29-30
Shallots 28, 109-110
Shrimp Meal 22
Small space gardening 1-2
Snails and slugs 34, 36, 39-40
Soil
  amending 13-14
  and roots 13
  beneficial microorganisms and bacteria 13, 16, 19
  clay i, 13-14
  drainage/testing 6, 14
  flooding 5-6
  for containers and raised beds 15
  loamy i
  mycorrhizae 17-18
  pH/checking 18-19
  potting 15-16, 18
  sandy 14
  salts in 5
Sorrel 111-112
Sowbugs 34, 36
Spider Mites 34, 40
Spinach 28, 89, 111, 113-114
  New Zealand 113
Spinosad 40
Spotted Wilt Virus 41, 78, 100
Sprouts 28, 47, 115-116
Squash 32-33, 47, 75, 103, 117-118
Stir-fry Greens (*see Greens for stir-fry*)
Sulfur 19, 21-22, 40-41, 76, 109, 118
Systemic Acquired Resistance (SAR) 17
Sudden Wilt 41, 104
Sun exposure 7-8
Sweet Potatoes, 28, 101
Swiss Chard 11, 81, 119-120

T
Temperature i, 1-2, 4-5, 7-11 17, 63, 69, 91, 95, 99, 105, 115-116, 124
  thermometer (outdoor) 8
Thrips 34, 39-40, 78, 100
Tobacco/Tomato Hornworm 34, 38
Tomatillos 121-122
Tomatoes 6, 8-10, 18, 24, 53, 77-78, 101, 121, 123-124, 128
  growing in winter 8-10
Transpiration 2
Trees 2, 8
Turnips 28, 85, 107, 125-126

V
Vermicomposting (*see worm castings*)
Vermiculite 16
Verticillium Wilt 41, 78, 100, 102, 104, 122, 124
Viruses 41, 78, 102

W
Watering
  and drought 1-3
  conservation 2-3
  gray water 2-3
  how to 3-4
  moisture meter 3-4
  overwatering 10-11, 20, 41
Weather fluctuations/unseasonable 4, 6, 8
Whiteflies 34, 39
Windy weather/Santa Ana windstorms 4-5
Worm castings/composting 16-17, 22, 38

Photo & Graphic Credits

Photos

Sabrina Wildermuth, Julie Bawden-Davis, Envato Elements, Dreamstime, Larissa Bahr

Sabrina Wildermuth: 29; 44-Jeremy Wildermuth; 46-47; 59; 64; 70; 73; 75; 84-85; 97; 119; 125

Julie Bawden-Davis: 15; 16; 27 bottom; 43; 54; 69

Envato Elements: Intro page-Lenorlv; 51-twenty20photos; 55-ivankmit; 63-viledevil; 72-DragonImages; 79-aetb; 87-vanillaechoes; 89-duskbabe; 93-Yakov_Oskanov; 95-AtlasComposer; 105-Rawpixel; 107-Mylitleye; 108-Kariklaustermeier; 109-charlotteLake; 112-Nikolaydonetsk; 117-nblxer

Dreamstime: 4-Bundit Minramun; 7-Fedecandoniphoto; 8-Pras Boonwong; 10-Fedecandoniphoto; 11-Zlikovec; 12-Maximiliane Wagner; 17-Phimchanok; 27 top-Nitsuki; 28-Lovelyday12; 30-Rustamank; 33-Dchapurin; 37 top-Mouskie; 37 bottom-Claffra; 41 top-Andrey Maximenko; 41 bottom-Yodke67; 82-twenty20photos; 96-Hse0193; 99-Iamtkb; 113-Christian Weiß; 115-chernetskaya; 121-Aas2009; 126-Bhofack2 130-Stevanovicigor

Larissa Bahr: 128

Graphics

Envato Elements: Dedication, Acknowledgments; Table of Contents; i; ii; 1; 12-13; 21; 22-23; 30-31; 40; 42; 43; 47-48; 50; 59; 62; 65; 66; 70-71; 78; 81; 83; 86; 88; 94; 100; 106; 108; 110; 112; 114; 127; 129; 131; 133; 134; end page

Southern California Vegetable Gardening

SoCal Year-Round Gardening Series

"The vegetable garden in SoCal. What a delight! Oodles of tasty, nutritious vegetables to plant and savor. Sun ripened tomatoes. Crunchy bell peppers. Cauliflower kissed by frost. Sweet peas straight off the vine popped into eager mouths. Lettuce crispy and full of flavor. All enjoyed under sunny skies in gardening paradise." - Mother Nature